Personal Best

Personal Best

STEP-BY-STEP COACHING FOR CREATING THE LIFE YOU WANT

David Rock

SIMON & SCHUSTER

AUSTRALIA

First published in Australia in 2001 by
Simon & Schuster (Australia) Pty Limited
20 Barcoo Street, East Roseville NSW 2069

A Viacom Company
Sydney New York London Toronto Singapore

National Library of Australia
Cataloguing-in-Publication data:

Rock, David
    Personal best: step-by-step coaching for creating the life
    you want.

    ISBN 0 7318 0970 X

    1. Life skills. 2. Self-actualisation (Psychology). 3.
    Success. 4. Self-help techniques I. Title

158.1

Cover design: Megan Ericcson
Internal design: Avril Makula GRAVITY AAD
Typeset in Berkeley 11 pt on 14 pt
Printed in Australia by Griffin Press

10 9 8 7 6 5 4

CONTENTS

ACKNOWLEDGMENTS

First I want to thank my wife Lisa Rock, without whom none of this would have been possible. When I first thought of the idea of coaching people for a living, Lisa believed in me enough to get me started. Thanks for putting up with my grouchy moods and late nights, and for doing most of the shopping, cooking, cleaning and housework (did I miss anything?) for four months while I focused on writing. You are an inspiration and the most wonderful partner.

My second big thanks goes to Tracy-Jean, my co-writer/partner/coach in this project. Thanks for your great writing, your awful deadlines and your brutally honest feedback. Tracy-Jean balances working as a Results coach, a writer and a radio presenter.

I also wish to thank my parents, Carole Sandberg and Sam Rock. Thanks for your unconditional love and support, and for allowing me to find my own path in life no matter how crazy it may have seemed at the time.

Thanks to Wendy Husband for telling me I should write a book, giving me the details of a publisher who would probably buy it if I did, then consistently following up to see what I had done about it. (Go coach!) Also thanks to Lyn Doolan for your read-through and editing, and to Megan Eriksson for your great cover design work on a tight deadline.

I am indebted to Roland Fishman from the Writers Studio for running such great writing classes, which I first attended in 1996. Your great coaching ('just keep the pen moving,' I hear you say) lit the way for me in many a dark hour at the keyboard.

Thanks to the board, management team, staff and all the coaches at Results without whom this story would have been very short. Your commitment to being of service to others has changed the lives of thousands people and continues to be a source of inspiration to me.

And finally, thanks to Julie Stanton and everyone at Simon & Schuster for seeing the potential in a book about coaching and being willing to give an unpublished author a go.

How It All Started

In 1996, after 10 years as a successful entrepreneur, I took time off to think about what I wanted to do next. Somehow word got out and before I knew it I had a dozen people asking me to help them get new ideas off the ground.

I started off as a bit of a consultant and mentor to lots of people. However, it quickly became obvious that people needed more than just advice to kick-start them in the direction of their dreams – they needed some kind of support structure to get them off the blocks and consistently hold them to their vision. They didn't need a consultant, they needed some kind of partnership.

Over 12 months of research and testing ideas I developed a system to do just that; a process that helped people get the results they wanted in their lives in a much faster way than they would on their own. It became clear early on that the system I had developed was just as effective for reducing stress, being a better manager, starting a relationship or getting healthy as it was for launching a new project. So I called it 'life coaching'. It was another 12 months before I found out that thousands of others around the world had started calling themselves life coaches too.

In 1997 I decided the system was so effective it should be available to a lot more people than I could ever coach by myself. Thus came the decision to train others to deliver it. This culminated in forming a company called Results Life Coaching and developing a one-year coach-training program.

Our first training program was delivered informally late in 1997. By 2000 we had trained over 150 people across Australia to become life coaches and opened our first franchise in the United States.

So far all this has resulted in over 1500 people being coached within a program we now call the Results Life Coaching System. Being coached under this system has positively and often dramatically impacted every one of these people's lives. Some people's stories sound almost like miracles; the person who starts a small business with the help of their coach and has more clients than they can handle within three months. Or the person who finds their life partner in just a few weeks. Other stories are more personal victories – like the person who finally starts taking responsibility for their happiness and gives up complaining about their life, or the person who gets their stress and time management under control and learns to say 'no'.

In 1999 I decided, with the prompting of several rather insistent coaches, that a book was in order to take this work out to an even wider audience. This book is the result of that decision.

THE PERSONAL COACHING SYSTEM

Most of us have had an experience of living at our personal best. It's a time when you see more solutions than problems, when life is exciting and challenging and you know you're living life as fully as you can. It might have been during some really testing time when your personal resources were stretched in some way, and you had to grow and develop as a person to meet the demands of the world around you. Or it might have been when you worked in a great partnership or team with someone that really excited and inspired you to push past your normal limitations. I know for me these times tend to be incredibly rewarding and fulfilling. They are times that make me smile when I think of them. They are also times of maximum growth and learning, times when we get to see ourselves in a new light, when we discover we are actually capable of more than we previously thought. These are the times we are performing at our personal best in our own lives.

Personal Best is designed to deliver this very experience. Put in very simple terms, it does this by helping people set powerful goals in their lives and then stick to them, over a three-month time frame.

The system works by drawing together the best elements from business, sports and personal development. In some ways it's like having a mentor, project manager, personal trainer and sports coach all rolled into one. Based on fundamental principles like integrity and accountability, the importance of emotional intelligence and a belief in human potential, the system has no base in any formal religion or ideology, though most of the themes in the system are to be found everywhere in the personal development movement.

What makes the system so powerful is not any major breakthrough or insight into human experience, but rather a breakthrough way of helping you *stay* on the path that most of us already know we want to be on – the path that has us achieve our personal best every day.

You might be thinking to yourself 'How can I get the experience of having a coach just from a book?' The answer, of course, is that you can't. However, the core elements of the 12-week journey that people go through when they undertake coaching are captured in this 12-chapter book. You get to go through a similar process to that of having a coach by following the stories, format and actions within the book. I'll talk more about this in the section 'Getting The Most Out Of This Book'.

For now I'd like to talk about some of the main principles that make this coaching system so effective.

IT'S ALL ABOUT YOU

I don't know about you, but I can be incredibly impatient when it comes to learning anything new. I really dislike sitting through even five minutes of a training program that's not 100 per cent relevant to me. That's one of the things that makes this book so powerful – it is completely focused on you, where you are at right now, your wants and needs, the results you want to get, and how you want to get them. It's not another preset training program based on other people's agendas for you. With this system, you are the expert in your own life; the coaching works to bring out the best in you.

You can use this system to work on anything important to you right now – to reduce your stress, get healthier, start a business, improve your relationships or just about anything you want to get new results in.

GETTING YOU FOCUSED ON SOLUTIONS INSTEAD OF PROBLEMS

This is not another system for working out all the things wrong with you. Ninety-nine per cent of us are incredibly tough on ourselves already, we know everything that could possibly be wrong with us, including many things that are not, so we certainly don't need any help in this area from anyone else.

Rather than looking at what your 'problems' are, in this book we focus on where are you now, where you want to be, what the best way to get there is, and what you are going to do about it – this week. By keeping our eye firmly focused on the solutions instead of the problems, lots of new possibilities open up. Along the way, as we start to get new results in our lives, we start to develop more self-confidence and self-awareness in areas that we thought were our weak spots. After a while these 'problem' areas seem to diminish on their own, without us having really focused on them directly at all.

STRETCHING IS GOOD FOR YOU

When was the list time you were encouraged to stretch yourself? Exhorted to be your best? Challenged to realise your potential? Dared to take a risk? There is just not enough of this in the world today. Many people spend their whole lives doing their best to avoid anything that might take them outside their comfort zone. Yet our most rewarding and fulfilling moments in life always seem to be when we are challenged in some way, not when everything is going along as normal.

I remember the Olympics in Sydney. It was one of the most emotional and inspiring times I have ever experienced. It was like New Year's Eve for three weeks, all the normal rules of life were on hold. People were nice to each other, they spoke to complete strangers on the street, they helped each other out. On the last night of the games, 1.5 million people jammed the city, and there were only a couple of incidents of any kind of violence, and no arrests. Imagine 1.5 million people jammed together for a night in your city being that well behaved.

What was the spirit that joined everyone together? I say it was everyone celebrating human potential, celebrating people stretching themselves to their limits, honouring people going for their 'personal best'. One of the most moving Olympic stories for me was about some runners from a Third World country who had worked for years to pay for their own travel to get to Sydney, and arrived with just the clothes on their back to compete in. And they were here to compete against the best in the world.

Personal Best helps you set inspiring and challenging goals, goals that will stretch you, goals that will focus your mind away from the ordinary events of everyday life, away from cynicism and resignation, and onto what is possible for your own future.

WE LOVE TO LEARN BUT HATE TO BE TAUGHT

Most of us like to learn things for ourselves. We don't always trust other people's advice, and often for good reason. The person giving us advice may be incorrect, or they may not have our real interests at heart, or they may be giving us advice that works well for them but wouldn't work for us. Watch your reaction next time someone gives you advice – do you accept it automatically?

One of the things that makes this book so effective is that no-one gives anyone any advice. Whether you only read this book or decide to take on a coach as well, you will always be choosing to take action on things of your own accord. You won't be told what you 'should' do. You do the learning, no-one will be teaching you or telling you what to do. This system is about speeding up the process of human learning, not giving you more external advice or knowledge.

KEEPING YOU FOCUSED ON YOUR GOAL

The system runs over 12 weeks, a time frame that is long enough to tackle really worthwhile projects, but short enough to stay focused and motivated.

Having a start, middle and end to the system provides a lot of 'traction' to the experience, meaning it gives the whole process of coaching some urgency and importance. I've noticed that I seem to give priority to the things that have a real deadline. Having a 90-day timeline, rather than just going into an ongoing coaching system, really does give your dreams a deadline, which in turn can spur you into action that much more.

SUCCESS IS ALMOST NEVER AN ACCIDENT

I've heard it said that success in life is simple: get a good plan and stick to it. Whether it's to lose weight, start a business or get a new job, when we get a good idea or set a big goal for ourselves, we usually tend to throw ourselves into it without taking the time to plan things properly. Often this means we end up doing things the way we always have, and therefore getting the same results we always have.

Personal Best will help you develop a step-by-step plan to achieve any goal. This plan breaks your goals down into 'do-able' bits, which helps you do what is often the hardest thing – get started!

The plan we have developed helps you think a lot more deeply about where you are right now in relation to your goal, what you really want by going for the goal, and what your true options for action are. It then helps you work out the best options for achieving your goals. By working with a step-by-step system like this you end up with a far richer plan for success than you've ever had before.

HELPING YOU STICK TO YOUR PLAN

At the start of every new year, millions of people around the world get excited about changing their lives and make new resolutions. How many of us keep them? We all lead very full lives, and unless we have something in place to continually remind us of our new resolutions, it's very easy to let it them slide.

You might have had an experience like this: you have a major realisation about something one day, maybe about exercising, and you absolutely resolve to do something about it; you are truly 100 per cent committed to it at the time. Then a little while later you wake up in a cold sweat and realise that not only have you forgotten about your decision, but you hardly care about it now, and wonder why you were so worked up about it before!

Becoming committed to new ideas is easy. Staying committed is the hard part. With so many things fighting for our attention these days, staying committed to anything requires support structures to help you when everything else comes and demands your attention.

My metabolism changed overnight when I hit 30. I went from being unable to put on weight no matter how much I ate, to gaining it fast no matter how little I ate. I was uncomfortable about it, a little shocked and confused, and even annoyed, to me it was some pesky problem that I didn't want to have to take responsibility for.

After a while I tried to do something about it on my own and decided to jog and start using the local gym. I did this a couple of times – over a month. Even though I was 'committed', other things kept getting in the way. Eventually I realised the only way I was going to exercise was if I took on personal trainer. Then I had to turn up. So I did. And it worked. After six months with my trainer I found I had enough momentum to keep exercising every week.

My point is, people don't need to know any more about how to live well. We already know everything we need to know about how to be fit, healthy, financially secure, in healthy relationships and happy. And if we don't know it, we can look it up in a book or on the Internet. Does having this knowledge make a lot of difference? Unfortunately, usually not. What makes a difference is taking action. And what makes a huge difference to taking action is having someone you are answerable to about your actions.

This book is not for people who just want to think more. It's for people who want results, who are ready for results, who have tried to get results on their own, and now recognise the importance of having a support structure to help them achieve their goals. This book will provide you with that weekly structure to help you stay on track.

MAKING 'YOU' THE PRIORITY

I know people who go for years without having one hour where they are their main priority. It's always their job, their partner, their family, the community or their sport, but not them.

Imagine what it would be like, just for three months, to make your success, your goals and dreams, your major priority. Making your life's goals more important than going to the movies, going drinking on the weekend or watching 'only' three hours a week of your favourite television shows. What could you do if you spent three hours a week committed to realising your potential? The system works partly because this is what people start to do. By having lofty goals and a structure for keeping them alive, suddenly *your* life, your vision, your goals become your main focus day-to-day. The changes that come about from this alone can be extraordinary.

BUILDING YOUR EMOTIONAL INTELLIGENCE

In his ground-breaking book, *Emotional Intelligence*, Daniel Goleman highlights the enormous impact that mastery of our emotions can have on our success in life. He actually found that all other things being equal, EQ was a stronger predeterminer of success in life than IQ or most other factors.

Coaching is a process that ultimately has us question our internal life and question our way of going about things. Many of the answers to these questions are to be found within our relationship with ourselves and others, the core of emotional intelligence competencies. As you will read throughout this book, coaching is a journey of self-exploration that builds our emotional intelligence to new levels.

Getting The Most From This Book

This book captures the 12 essential steps that give you an experience like that of having your own coach.

The way to get the most value from the book is to use it as a real workbook for your life, reading one chapter a week for 12 weeks and doing all the actions you come up with each week. The book weaves together stories of three clients going through the 12 steps, to help you see and feel what it's like to go through each stage of the system. While you will probably get lots of insights just by reading the stories, the real value of this book will come from doing the actions and acting as if the book is your coach.

If you want to get even more value from the book, read it each week with a good friend. You can do this in person or even on the phone. Coaching is surprisingly effective by phone, as there are often far fewer distractions.

Whether you are going to read this alone or with a friend, put aside a regular time to read the book each week, for example every Monday night at 7 pm. Block this time out in your diary for the next 90 days so nothing else can get in the way. Make sure you choose a time when you can be completely undistracted, by your children or other events going on.

You will need one to two hours every week to read the chapter of the book and work out your actions. The other time you need will depend on what you take on at the end of each chapter, but I would suggest that a minimum of one extra hour each week will be required – this will vary dramatically according to the goal.

Look through other things coming up in the next 90 days. Be realistic but also be prepared to push yourself and feel a little uncomfortable. Many coaching clients have had to give up TV watching for the duration of their coaching series to transform their lives – a small price to pay.

For now, let's get started with the first step in coaching – setting yourself some goals.

Set A Goal Worth Going For

We need to learn to set our course by the stars, not by the lights of every passing ship.

OMAR NELSON BRADLEY

Olympic athletes achieve their personal best when they are competing with a real goal in mind – usually it's going for the gold. Imagine if the Olympics didn't have any medals involved, or worse, if they had no way of measuring who had won any of the events. I'd say the world record times would be a little lower than they are now.

It's the same in life. Getting to your personal best performance requires you to have an inspiring, visionary goal to pull you forward, to draw the best out of you. It requires that you have a 'goal worth going for'.

What's the difference between this kind of goal and the ones we normally set in life? Most of the goals people tend to have already are things like 'to be a millionaire by 21', 'to retire at 40', 'to lose lots of weight', or 'to travel the world for a year'. Are these goals worth going for? Well, yes, they would be, if we achieved them. But how many of us actually achieve these kinds of goals? I'd say not very many, or else there would be a few billion millionaires travelling the world at 40!

Perhaps we set unrealistic goals, or we don't take them seriously enough, who knows. I can't give you the answer to that. What I can give you is a way to set goals for yourself that can truly change your life.

'Goals worth going for' are almost always different from the kind of goals people set on their own. They also tend to be different from what you may have learned in management courses, training workshops or other self-help books.

It's not just about making sure your goals are specific and measurable, although it's generally best if goals do have these qualities. It's not just about making sure the goals are achievable either. In fact, as you read on, you'll discover that some of the very best goals are ones that we have absolutely no idea how to achieve. At the same time, it's not just about setting enormous goals either. If we don't believe, on some level, that a goal is at least possible, we won't really take serious action towards achieving it – and thus we won't make it a priority.

Setting goals worth going for is something new altogether. It's an art that once mastered will alter the course of your future. Having a goal worth going for changes the fabric of your every waking hour. It alters how you feel, think and act, and makes your world a bigger place.

Let's have a look at how I helped three clients set goals worth going for, and then come back and look at how to set these kinds of goals for yourself. Many of the clients' details have been changed to protect confidentiality, otherwise the stories are based on composites of stories of real clients I have worked with over the last few years.

Before I start, I'd like to say something about the kind of conversations you will read that I have had with people in the stories that follow. They are quite unusual; some people might think they are so unusual they are untrue. However, they are exactly the kind of conversations that occur every day in coaching sessions. What makes them so unusual is the quality of the relationship that occurs between a client and a coach.

When people ask me to coach them, they expect several things. In fact they are paying me specifically to do these things. They expect me to:

- encourage and believe in them 100 per cent;
- see things about them that they can't see about themselves, and they expect me to tell the truth about this;
- ask them the hard questions; and
- hold them to their word.

This is certainly an uncommon type of relationship in the course of ordinary life. These expectations are at the root of what makes coaching such an effective and powerful process for forwarding people's learning journey. If you've ever experienced the power of someone believing in you 100 per cent you'll know just what I mean.

So if you are choosing to work with a partner as you go through this book, I challenge you to take on these same expectations from each other. As you read the stories and listen to me coaching the people in them, you will get a good sense of how to do that.

Melissa was a junior account manager in a large public relations firm in Sydney. She was 28 when she heard about me from a friend and called up about some career coaching.

Melissa turned up to our first session with a black leather notepad and gold pen at the ready. She had an open, kind face, with long, dark hair tied up at the back. I asked her where she was at in her career right now.

'I started out doing basic stuff to get in on the ground floor, being a bit of a PA, arranging meetings and doing all the photocopying,' she said. 'A couple of years back we had a big deadline when our account managers were away, so I went home one night and thought up some ideas for a rough campaign and showed my boss the next morning. He seemed to like it, because from that day on I've been writing various campaigns for all sorts of clients, though I'm still only called a junior account manager.'

'Sounds like you've got great "get up and go" for your job, so what's bothering you so much about your career?'

'The thing is, I'm the main writer now on accounts that are bringing in thousands of dollars a day. I'm working sometimes 70 hours a week, doing all the real work, and you know what? I'm only getting $28,000 a year.'

I asked her what was bothering her most, the hours, the pay, the need for more respect, or that she could be doing this herself.

'It's not really the money you know,' she paused and let out a sigh. 'It's just that I do the real work, so I feel I should have more ... I don't know ... something.'

'Recognition?' I added gently.

'No, it's more than that. I do want more recognition, but it's also more respect, more control and, yes, I wouldn't say no to more money, but that's not that main thing.'

I was getting a sense of where she was heading.

'It sounds to me almost like you want to be running your own show?' I suggested.

'Exactly,' she replied, closing her folder loudly. It was like a light had just gone on in her head. 'I suppose that's been in the back of my mind for a while and I wanted to talk to you about it.'

'So what's stopping you? Why don't you just go and do it?'

'Easy for you to say, I'm not sure I can ...' She stopped mid-sentence.

We were starting to get close to the core issue – to set a goal worth going for.

'So Melissa, do you want to work with me on getting your new business started?'

'I guess I do, it's just pretty scary, I've never done anything like that on my own.'

I asked her what kind of goal we should set, as a focus for three months of working together. 'What about "to be ready to start my own business"?' she offered.

I suggested we look at something more tangible and specific: 'How would you know you had started your own business?'

'Well, I suppose I would have to have an office, but I already work from home, so that's not an issue, and I would need to stop working where I am, and I'd need a few clients.'

'So what about a goal focused on getting clients?' I suggested.

Melissa face went a little white. 'Wow,' she replied, looking up at the ceiling. 'That would be incredible. I was thinking about doing it sometime in the next year. Having clients in three months ... that would be big.'

'So are you willing to go for it?' I asked.

'I guess that's what I want, I'm just a bit nervous.'

I checked to make sure she felt it was an achievable goal, and she assured me the main things in the way were just confidence, focus and commitment. All that was left now was to decide how many clients to go for, to give the goal a real measure. I suggested five.

'Are you nuts?' she replied. 'I can see myself getting maybe a couple at the most.'

'Great, so what about going for three?' I said, with a grin.

She hesitated, then her face lit up a little too. 'Why not. I guess it's time I stopped thinking about it and started getting serious. Let's go for three clients within three months.'

Now we had a goal worth going for. This goal certainly changed the very fabric of her life, it had her thinking differently about herself, about her capabilities and got her more inspired than she'd ever been. Compare that to a goal she might have set on her own, like 'to be ready to start a business', or 'to know what I want to do next'.

So what qualities did this goal have? For a start, it focused on her real dream, not just something small like getting a promotion or more money. This is one of the keys to setting a goal worth going for – the goal has to be something we really value, something we dream of having, something that would truly change our life if we achieved it.

So we set a goal around a dream, we gave it a 90-day deadline, we made sure it was more challenging than any Melissa would have tackled on her own, that it was achievable, snappy, and had a measure. But most of all we made sure it was something positive, uplifting and visionary that would be coursing through her veins for the next few months.

Let's look at how I helped another client set goals for himself.

Mike was a senior manager in a large consulting firm. He was 45 and married with two young children.

Mike had heard about coaching through his company, who had offered to pay for any coaching their senior staff wanted. His wife had suggested he look into it after he had been complaining for several months about stress at work.

Mike turned up at my office for our first session in a well-cut navy pinstriped suit. He told me he was in charge of a division of 100 staff that handled large IT projects. The team sold and installed software for several of the big banks and tele-communications firms, projects usually worth tens of millions of dollars.

I asked Mike what was happening in his work right now.

'Oh, everything's going along pretty smoothly, no major dramas,' he replied.

'So what would you like to work on with me then?' I asked.

'I just want some ideas for how to get my division going a bit, to get my team a bit more motivated. Some of them are good, but a lot of them ... ' – he looked to the side, checking out the titles in my bookcase – 'kind of don't care much. They're out of there at one minute past five every day, if you know what I mean.'

We talked about the value of goals, and how I liked my clients to have specific goals. I asked Mike if there was a goal the team was working on together.

'Well, I have a bit of a target, more like a budget really, but the team doesn't have much input in that, I just have to knock them into shape to make it happen.' He looked me in the eye and lowered his voice a little. 'Are you suggesting that we should have a goal for the whole team?'

'Well maybe. It would need to be your goal, but working with the team might be part of how you tackle it,' I replied.

'You know what, that's not such a bad idea at all.'

We discussed this idea for a few minutes and played around with a few alternatives until Mike decided this was the best option. I asked him what kind of target he wanted to set.

> 'I like the idea of getting sales back to where they were this time last year. We've dropped a lot since then.'
>
> 'Do you think that would inspire everyone?' I asked tentatively.
>
> 'Hmmm. Well, maybe not. What do you suggest?'
>
> I thought for a few seconds. 'What about pitching it at a specific dollar value, perhaps something you haven't achieved before, something that would give everyone a good feeling of achievement?'
>
> 'Sounds fair enough,' he replied. 'Like what?'
>
> 'Well, what's your best sales figure in three months so far?'
>
> 'About $5 million. We could go for $6 million, that'd be a bit of a stretch.'
>
> 'What about 10?' I threw in straight away.
>
> 'Ten!' he exclaimed. 'We're only budgeting 10 for most of this year, I'd probably get a damn good bonus if we got that.'
>
> 'Is it achievable, do you think, in three months?' I asked.
>
> 'Well, if even half the sales people did what our top few do, it would be easy,' he replied.

We discussed the feasibility of this as a goal and I made sure it tied in with his corporate responsibilities and objectives, and that he had the resources to pull it off. Once all this was confirmed, we agreed on the goal of '$10 million in new business'. Mike said he felt really inspired about the goal, and although he had no idea how he would achieve it yet, he said he was willing to go for it 100 per cent.

For Mike the key to setting a goal worth going for was to be stretched, to give him something that would get his creative juices flowing again. Sometimes we need to set goals that are way outside of our current paradigm to help kick-start ourselves into any form of change.

I met Jan while shopping at one of my favourite menswear stores in the city. She was in her mid-thirties, with short blonde hair and a raucous laugh. Jan asked me what I did for a living while I was trying on some new suits for spring. I told her I was a life coach. 'That's exactly what I need,' she piped up enthusiastically. I offered to give her a free trial coaching session and she accepted immediately.

Our first session felt like we had known each other for years already. I asked her what she most wanted from coaching. 'I want to start having more fun, I seem to just work, work and do nothing else, except look after my daughter. Sometimes on the weekends I go out with friends, but not much else ever happens. I'm ready for something new.'

> 'Like what?' I asked.
> 'I don't know. If I did I wouldn't need you!' she joked.
> 'So what's happening in the romance department then?' I'd had an inkling this was the thing missing for her.
> 'Oh, please, don't go there, it's all too hard.'

It took another 10 minutes for Jan to admit to herself she had given up on the idea of having a relationship. At the same time she admitted to me that she did really want one, but didn't feel ready.

After several more minutes of discussion we ended up with a goal 'to be in the best relationship ever'. Jan said she felt mildly ill at the idea but acknowledged that this was the thing that was most missing in her life, this was the thing that would make the most difference to her if she got results in it.

For those of you wondering, relationship goals are great things to work on within this system, and often with amazing results. Though not every person meets Mr or Ms Right in three months, by working systematically on this area, making it a priority and putting some quality thinking time into it, we almost always see some kind of positive result.

So what else is there to learn from Jan's goals? Notice that the core issue was not the obvious one on the surface – Jan thought she just wanted more fun in her life, a life outside her work. Yet what she really wanted was to be in a relationship again. Often it seems like the answer to all our prayers is just to have more fun, be more productive, get more organised or learn to manage time better. Yet sometimes it's more important to manage what's going on underneath that – things like our health, relationship or financial issues.

Often the goals we set in life only further our struggles, increase our stress or make us harder on ourselves, instead of helping us along the path to being happier and more fulfilled in our day-to-day lives.

A goal worth going for is one that focuses on the issue that will make the most difference to you. What you can see from these stories is the real core issue is often not the obvious answer. Sometimes it takes a lot of self-honesty to see what it is that is *really* worth going for in your life, and to be willing to go for it as a goal.

Action Station

I'll now take you through a step-by-step process to set the goal you will be working with for the duration of this book.

If you're not sure of the general area you'd like to set a goal in, the next exercise will help you. If you are already clear on the area, go to the section called 'Focus on the core issue'.

GETTING CLEAR ON WHERE TO SET A GOAL

There's a list below of all the areas people tend to want to set goals in. This list will be referred to in future action stations, so any goal area you choose to set your goal in will be supported all the way through this book.

Look over the list and put a tick next to five areas that seem to be most important to you right now.

Once you have five, look at your shortlist closely and ask yourself this question: which area would make the least difference to you if you had a big shift in it? Put a line through that area. Keep doing this until you are left with just one area. This is the area that will have the most impact on your life once your goal is achieved.

If you are having trouble choosing, look for the way that an improvement in one area could cause a change in another.

For example, if you have to choose between finance and career, ask yourself – if I had a new job, would my finances be taken care of? If the answer is yes, then the less important of the two would be finances. Alternatively, if having more money saved meant that you would be able to start your dream business, then career would be less important at this time.

Finances
- Save money
- Get out of debt

Business
- Start a new business
- Build my current business

Relationships
- Start a new relationship
- Improve an existing relationship

Health
- Increase my fitness
- Increase my energy levels
- Resolve a medical issue

Personal
- Decrease stress
- Increase confidence
- Increase personal satisfaction, happiness, joy or fun

Career
- Find a new job
- Improve my work performance

Creative
- Complete a creative project
- Develop my creativity

SETTING YOUR GOAL

There are a few key rules for setting inspiring goals. If you follow these and the examples, you should have something great to work with. Let's look through these rules now.

FOCUS ON THE CORE ISSUE

Look at the area you have chosen and brainstorm all of the different issues going on for you in that area at this time. Get a clean sheet of paper (paper is better than computer for this kind of exercise) and start writing down all the issues that come to mind.

Keep on writing until you have nothing left to add. Then use a process of elimination, as above, considering which issue would have the least impact within that area at this time, until you have found the core issue.

Many choices at this stage of coaching rely on intuition and it is important that you start listening to yours – give yourself a quiet space and take your time to uncover the core issue. If you are not sure straight away, take a break for a few days then come back to it.

Consider Melissa's story again about how she reached her goal. Notice how she knew she wanted to change something about her career, but she was focusing on her current job only. When I suggested that she consider working for herself she realised that her goal should be focused on her own business instead. Sometimes we need to think outside the square of our normal thoughts to find the core issue.

Doing a brainstorm exercise is an opportunity for you to write down everything you are thinking or feeling about something – in this case, a specific goal area. Try to not re-read the list until you have absolutely nothing left to write. It can be a private document that you don't want to share with anyone else, so include every thought – even the ones that make you feel fear or embarrassment. The aim is to have it all down in front of you, on paper. Here is an example of what a brainstorm may look like:

GOAL AREA: HEALTH – TO INCREASE MY FITNESS
ISSUES GOING ON AT THIS TIME IN THAT AREA:
Aging
Don't know if I have the money to put towards equipment
Don't own any jogging shoes
Feel embarrassed by how I look
Heavier now than I have ever been
Have tried heaps of stuff before with no result
Don't trust myself to follow through
It's too hard
I don't want to focus on my eating
I don't like exercise
I know I need to look after myself
I want to do this for my children

Reading back over this list the client realises that she has many excuses why she has been putting off getting fit (no shoes, no money, doesn't like exercise, too hard, feeling embarrassed, don't trust myself) and also some very good reasons for being fit (aging, need to look after herself, her children, heaviest she has ever been). After grouping all of these things together she sees that her reasons for doing it outweigh the excuses, even though there are more excuses, and that the one reason that stands out is her children. We then decided to focus the goal around that and it ends up as 'to play a whole game of football with the kids'. As you can see from this example, you may need to open up your thoughts and think laterally to uncover what the core issue is for you.

DEFINE THE GOAL AS A 90-DAY PROJECT

I have found that 90 days is enough time to really make an impact on people's lives, but short enough to maintain motivation and excitement.

Get out your diary and actually count out 90 days, marking when the goal will be complete. Look at the time span in front of you. Feel the power of having that as a deadline. Focus on how your life could change for the better if you used the next 90 days to achieve a goal worth going for.

Also consider that you will be totally committing these 90 days to achieving that goal – is it really something that is that important to you? If not, go back to the categories and come up with a different goal.

The goal you create now can be part of a bigger goal, but the actual goal you'll choose here needs to be focused just on this next 90 days. It's too easy to avoid starting when a goal is too big – with three-month goals at least you are taking real action in the direction you want to go in. For example, if you have a long-term goal to run a marathon, perhaps your three-month goal is to run 10 kilometres in under an hour. Or perhaps you want to be financially independent – what could you do in the next 90 days as part of that? Maybe you could save $5000, or make your first investment on the stock market or clear all credit card debt.

It is also more powerful for the goal to read as some kind of project, not just something you want. For example 'give out 50 new business cards' is a project, and is probably going to be a stronger goal than 'start a new business'. It is generally easier to work towards a project that has a real conclusion, some kind of event or action, than it is to work towards something conceptual. Want to be more creative? Instead of a goal of 'enjoy my creativity more', try setting a goal around having an exhibition, even if it's only for your own family to attend!

BE OPEN TO BEING REALLY CHALLENGED

Go for a goal that you don't know for sure you can do, something that makes you a little excited and nervous at the same time. In fact, the best goal is one you don't know how you're going to achieve, you just sense you'll be able to work it out if you really apply yourself.

I know that might sound odd, but the fact is, if you know exactly how you're going to achieve a goal, you're likely to just do things the way you always have. You won't be stretching yourself, learning new skills or developing new habits, which are some of the aims of coaching. So go for a goal that makes your belly turn ever so slightly.

Consider Melissa in the story above, and how she reacted to hearing me suggest a goal of having her first three clients in three months. Of course to her it seemed big and she thought she had no idea how to do it, but it wasn't out of her realm of possibility. Going for three clients rather than just one made a big difference to her in the end – it had her thinking much bigger and believing in herself more.

A great way to see how much you can challenge yourself is to take the written goal and up the ante, then observe your reactions. For example, you may have a goal to have a savings plan – what if you changed it to 'have $1000 invested' then say you still felt that wasn't challenging enough when you considered your finances and the 90 days ahead. Increase the measure again to 'have $5000 invested'. That should elicit some kind of reaction. Go for something with some stretch.

MAKE SURE IT IS ACHIEVABLE

As well as challenging you to stretch, the goal must also be achievable for you within the next 90 days. It is important to ensure that the goal you set for yourself is not *too* big. A goal that is set too high can overwhelm you rather than motivate you. For example, if your goal is 'to be debt-free' but you currently owe $100,000 on your mortgage, you may be setting yourself up to fail rather than challenging yourself with your goal. What you could do instead is set a goal like 'having an extra $10,000 paid off my mortgage' or 'reducing my personal debt by 30 per cent'.

The point is, if you don't truly believe a goal is achievable, you won't get serious about it.

I once coached a client who had a goal 'to pass all of my uni exams with flying colours'. However, she hadn't put enough work in during the start of the year to really have that goal happen to her satisfaction. Instead, she spent week after week in our sessions beating herself up over how much study she should have done while actually doing very little. Having this unachievable goal turned into a way for her to set herself up to fail. Sometimes you might start out with a goal that you think is achievable, then a few weeks into it you realise it isn't. It's okay to change your goals at that time. Just don't trudge along pretending to go for a goal that inside you truly know is not possible. People change their goals all the time, there's nothing wrong with giving something all you've got, then discovering you need to change course mid-stream.

MAKE IT SNAPPY

The goal you choose is going to be your motivation for change, and you're going to be saying it to yourself over and over again during these next 90 days. So keep it short and snappy. You don't need to say everything in the goal itself. The best goals are around five words, not long statements. You need to make the goal memorable to you so that it stays at the front of your mind.

Make sure you tailor the goal to what will excite you. Some of us respond well to visual images. If the image has an emotional subtext, even better. To get a goal that's really worth going for, try to capture some kind of visual element in the goal, for example 'fit my best jeans' is stronger than 'be a size 8'. Or 'crack open champagne at the launch' is better than 'start a new business'. Consider other senses as well. Maybe you want to 'live where I can smell the ocean' or 'hear my song played on the radio'.

The following are examples of good goals, followed by the same goal that has been made snappy in some way:

Finances
Save money
- To have $5000 in the bank
- To pay cash for my new car

Get out of debt
- To be debt-free
- To love my bank statements

Business
Start a new business
- To open my business
- To have 100 satisfied customers worldwide

Build my current business
- To improve turnover by 100 per cent
- To read my name in *Fortune*

Relationships
Start a new relationship
- To be in a great relationship
- To feel like a lovesick teenager

Improve an existing relationship
- To be more in love with my partner
- To get married

Health
Increase my fitness
- To run the City to Surf
- To run alongside Steve Monaghetti

Increase my energy levels
- To feel more energised
- To leap out of bed every day

Resolve a medical issue
- To feel well
- To be glowing with good health

Personal
Decrease stress
- To feel less stressed
- To have every day feel like a Sunday

Increase confidence
- To speak up more
- To give a public speaking engagement

Increase personal satisfaction, happiness, joy or fun
- To feel better about life
- To cry with laughter at least once a day

Career
Find a new job
- To start my dream job
- To have my name up in lights

Improve my work performance
- To get noticed at work
- To love being at work

Creative
Complete a creative project
- To display my paintings
- To have people bidding for my works

Develop my creativity
- To practise music diligently
- To hear applause after a public performance

THE TREASURE OF A MEASURE

The measure of the goal is the element of the goal that is going to let you know when you have achieved the goal or how close you are. I cannot stress enough how important it is to have an accurate, objective measure. A measure can be related to another time in your life ('to be as fit as I was in high school'), a percentage ('to be 50 per cent fitter'), a numeric scale ('to be an 8 out of 10 in my fitness') or a physical outcome ('to wear a size 10' or 'to fit my favourite jeans'). It is important that the measure is written into the goal so that you hear it every time you read the goal. To help you out, imagine someone else reading your goal – how would they be able to tell that you had achieved it? Sometimes getting the measure can be the hard bit – if you can't get it first off, come back to it after a few days with a fresh mind.

A FINAL TEST – DOES THE GOAL TRULY INSPIRE YOU?

Once you've taken the above into consideration it is time to write your goal. Below are a list of 'okay' goals and a list of 'great' goals. If you get stuck, refer to these to help you along. It is okay for you to use one of these goals if you really feel that it fits exactly where you are at.

Finances
Save money
- Okay: To start a savings plan
- Great: $10,000 in the bank

Get out of debt
- Okay: To stop spending
- Great: Credit cards at zero

Business
Start a new business
- Okay: To stop being an employee
- Great: My name on the door

Build my current business
- Okay: To increase turnover
- Great: $10,000 a month in sales

Relationships
Start a new relationship
- Okay: To meet someone new
- Great: Be in the most romantic relationship ever

Improve an existing relationship
- Okay: To make things better with my spouse
- Great: As in love with my partner as when we first met

Health

Increase my fitness
- Okay: To lose 5 kilograms
- Great: Have the physique of a teenager

Increase my energy levels
- Okay: To feel more energised
- Great: Have as much energy as my son

Resolve a medical issue
- Okay: To stop smoking
- Great: Twice as healthy as I've ever been

Personal

Decrease stress
- Okay: To feel calmer
- Great: Stress levels at 3/10

Increase confidence
- Okay: To speak out more
- Great: Be twice as confident as I've ever been

Increase personal satisfaction, happiness, joy or fun
- Okay: To laugh more
- Great: Have the most fun three months of my life

Career

Find a new job
- Okay: To work somewhere good
- Great: Land my dream job

Improve my work performance
- Okay: To improve my performance in my job
- Great: Promoted to senior consultant

Creative

Complete a creative project
- Good: To complete shooting the film
- Great: Show my work on the big screen

Develop my creativity
- Okay: To finish writing my story
- Great: Have my first short story published

When looking at your goal and reading it to yourself, you should feel some kind of physical response. As with Jan, it may be nausea, or it may make you want to punch the air.

If not, consider whether the goal is really something that you want to achieve at this time in your life. Are you willing to commit the next 90 days to make this happen? Does it inspire you to your core?

If you are sure that the goal is in the right area but still doesn't hit hard enough, look at the elements of your goal one by one. Is it challenging enough? Perhaps it's too big and not achievable. Consider your measure – is it something that really motivates you? Is the goal just written clumsily? It is quite common to get the goal slightly wrong the first time you write it down. Compare it to the examples given in this book or show it to your coaching friend. Write the goal and go back to it after a few days' break – does it still have an impact on you? Creating a goal worth going for is a process that takes time – don't expect to get it right straight away. It really is worth taking the time now to get it right as this is what you will be focusing on for the next 90 days of your life.

My goal worth going for is:

_____

_____

Where Are You Now, Really?

Reality isn't the way you wish things to be, nor the way they appear to be, but the way they actually are.

ROBERT J. RINGER

When you set off on a long journey of any kind, it helps if you know where you are before you start. That way you know the best path to follow, how far you have to go to get to your destination, what the journey will be like along the way, what challenges you are likely to face as you go and what supplies you might need.

It's the same with achieving your goals. Now that you have an exciting destination to head towards, a goal worth going for, you need to take time to find out everything about your current position in relation to this goal. How close are you to achieving it already? What are your resources for achieving it? What is your track record of success so far in this area? That is, what have you tried before and has worked, or hasn't worked, in relation to this goal?

Answering these questions thoroughly will deliver valuable insights into how you can achieve your goals more effectively than you may have in the past. Just this step alone can increase your chances of success many times over. Not doing this can undermine any great strategy you might come up with.

The 'Where Are You Now, Really?' stage is also the first time you will be taking action to start to bring your goals to life. In this step you may well be thinking more honestly and truthfully about your current position than you ever have before.

There are two things to be aware of in this stage:

1. It may help you to know that nearly everyone at this stage experiences a sense of resistance to finding things out. For some reason, most of us don't like finding out the truth about our current situation in relation to any of our goals. It might be fear of finding out things we don't like, or just an underlying desire to stay in our comfort zone. Have you ever noticed how much you avoid being honest about what you eat if you go on a diet? Or if you're struggling with your finances, that the last thing you are willing to do is sit down and work out your income and expenses? I know for myself when I wanted to get more fit, I tried my best to avoid being honest with myself about how much exercise I was really doing.

2. The good news is that finding out the truth of where you are in relation to your goal is almost always an immensely rewarding experience. You'll find out things that will make your goal seem even closer. For example, how many resources you already have for achieving your goal. Also, we don't make a habit of acknowledging what we already have, we tend to take our past success for granted. I remember a client who wanted to write a book and thought he was years away from being able to do it, till he found out he already had an agent, co-writer and lots of the material on hand, when he looked more closely. Sometimes even the bad news is good, as you no longer have to fear the unknown. I have experienced this myself in the past – it's much more stressful not knowing your financial position, than it is knowing exactly what your debts are.

So 'Where Are You Now, Really?' is a vital stage in the steps to realising your goal, and one that you should tackle with as much verve and gusto as setting your goal. Let's look at what happened when my three clients went through this step.

Melissa had expected to be years away from being able to start a business. When we discussed how she could 'get real' with her situation, Melissa decided to write out an honest list of at least 25 resources she already had to start a business.

To me, her list looked like the list of someone just about ready to open their door for business. The home office was already in place, with a phone, printer/fax/copier, computer, and an Internet connection. She had a list of six skills: 'being a good writer, understanding strategy, great at pitching ideas, good with finding opportunities, excellent under pressure, and loves a challenge.' She also listed 10 great business contacts that she felt would be willing to hear her pitch.

I asked her what she had learned from doing the list.

'You know what, I'd never seen this before,' she replied, 'but I think I have almost everything I need, except maybe bookkeeping, but I suppose I can learn that fairly easily. I think maybe in the back of my mind I knew I was ready, but didn't want to admit it to myself ... then I mightn't have any more excuses for not doing it. Funny thing is, I actually feel relieved, lighter somehow, not more afraid.'

Melissa found that getting real could be an inspiring and rewarding experience that frees up a lot of energy for other things. Now she could see it was possible, Melissa set off to visualise what her life would be like in her own business, the next step in moving towards her goal.

Mike had decided to do a thorough analysis of where he was at in relation to getting $10 million of new business this quarter. He listed how much new business he was already expecting. He did an analysis by computer of the performance of his sales team to see how they were tracking. All of this took only a few minutes to do but was worth a fortune in insights.

I asked him what he had discovered.

'Well, you know, I had expected we would have about two or three million in confirmed sales already, but it turns out we only have just over $1 million. I think I'd been basing my thoughts on what our overly optimistic sales people were telling me in the canteen, instead of checking orders in the system. I also worked out that four of the sales people are bringing in more results than the other 11 put together, which was a bit of a surprise. I almost wanted to fire half of the slack ones on the spot when I worked this out. The only good news I got was we had a lot more leads and enquiries than I'd expected, we just haven't been getting out to them fast enough to close the deals.'

'Sounds like good news to me,' I said seriously.

'Not sure I follow you,' he replied.

'Well, the thing is, now you have a chance to do something about all this, rather than find out about this problem later, or worse, be told by your superiors.'

'Look, the thing is, now I've seen this, I really have to do something about setting it right, right now. Do you think I should cull some of the slacker ones, or maybe give them minimum targets each week, or maybe just a warning? What do you reckon?'

I took a deep breath and let it out slowly before speaking. 'Can I give you my honest opinion, something I'm not sure you are going to like?'

'Shoot.'

'I think the thing you most need to do is to wait, do some more research, get a clearer picture of what's going on and how you can best impact things, find out all your options. To rush in now before you do this might not give you the result you want.'

Mike was a little uncomfortable with this but eventually agreed to hold back and let the next few weeks of the coaching process take their course.

When Jan went through the process of finding out where she was in relation to her goal, she realised she had only been dating one or two people a year since her last relationship had ended four years ago. This was a vital piece of information. Suddenly, instead of feeling like it was something that would never happen because it was 'too hard', Jan was able to see the real cause of why she wasn't meeting anyone interesting. Not only was she doing nothing about dating, she was doing nearly everything she could to avoid meeting men that might like her. Getting real with herself about what she was doing now about this goal was the first step to making it all the more possible.

Action Station

There is an exercise I'd like to give you now that is worth doing every week before you set new actions for yourself. This exercise gives you the opportunity to check in on how you are relating to your goal at this time. Once a week, when you work with this book, you will make a note, one or two words is enough, about how you are feeling in relation to your goal this week. You could be feeling anything from excited, to annoyed, to 'I just forgot'. One of the reasons this is important is that at the end of the 90-day process, you'll look back and see not only how far you've come, but that you moved forward no matter what you were feeling about the goal at the time. This is an important skill to learn and apply to all areas of your life.

How are you feeling/thinking about your goal this week? Say the words of your goal out loud to yourself right now, then write down one or two words that capture how you are feeling about your goal in the space below.

How I feel about this goal is:

_____

_____

_____

_____

HOW TO USE THE ACTION STATIONS

Every action station from now on will include suggested actions called 'possible actions', that may be grouped by goal area, and in some cases further specified by the issues that commonly fall under those areas. If you are serious about moving forward, take on as many of the possible actions as you feel are appropriate to where you are at. Generally this should be between two and four actions for your goal every week.

It is important that you take note of the actions you agree to do at the end of each reading session, so that you can see where you are progressing and to gain insights as you go along. There may be actions you think of which are more appropriate than the examples provided. If this is the case, go for it – one of the best moments in a coaching series is when a client takes over and starts writing their own actions. The important thing to remember when writing actions is that they must be as specific as possible so that you know without a doubt when the action has been completed. For example, 'to write a list of things about my current job' is not as specific as 'to write a list of 15 things I love and 15 things I hate about my current job'. Write the action(s) you are going to do in the space provided at the end of each chapter.

SET NEW ACTIONS

It's time to set yourself some homework that will help you uncover the truth of your position in relation to your goal. Your aim is to arm yourself with all the information that is available about your current situation. Like Mike or Jan, this process may only take a few minutes or it may be a matter of allocating some time for more thorough research. Whatever the case, give yourself enough time so that you really know what's going on for you at this time. I suggest you take a week to complete this action station.

POSSIBLE ACTIONS

Finances
Save money
Get out of debt
- Assess your current financial situation – write a balance sheet including income and expenses, assets, debts, balances of your bank accounts.
- Write down everything you spend this week.

- Write down all major expenses coming up in the next 12 months.
- Make a list of everything you use your credit card for.

Business
Start a new business
- Write a thorough inventory of at least 30 things that you have to start – include skills, resources and contacts.
- Write a list of anything missing to start your own business.
- Collate all the work you have put in to starting your own business right now.
- Write a SWOT analysis (strengths, weaknesses, opportunities, threats) of your new business.

Build my current business
- Complete an up-to-date profit and loss statement for the business.
- Identify all of your current sources of income.
- Identify your top five clients.
- Write an assessment of your role in improving the business.

Relationships
Start a new relationship
- Write the top three things you got out of previous relationships.
- Write a list of 20 pluses and 20 minuses about you as a potential partner.
- Write a page outlining all your beliefs or thoughts that you still carry around with you from previous relationships that might be hindering you now.
- Write a page on what you think you bring to a relationship.

Improve an existing relationship
- Write a list of 20 things about your partner that first attracted you to him/her.
- Write a list of 20 things about your partner that attract you now.
- Write a list of 10 activities you used to do together that you both enjoyed.
- Keep note in your diary of how much time during the week that you currently commit to your relationship.

Health
Increase my fitness
Increase my energy levels
Resolve a medical issue
- Get a full medical.
- Go for a fitness assessment at the gym.
- Write a list of everything you eat this week.
- Make a note of how much sleep you get this week and how energised you feel each day out of a rating of 1 to 10.

Personal
Decrease stress
- Make a note in your diary of everything that makes you feel stressed this week.
- Make a list of 10 things that currently decrease your stress and indicate how much time you spend doing them each week.
- Make a list of all the things you do each week to look after yourself.
- Make a list of 10 things you have done in the past that de-stressed you.

Increase confidence
- Make a note in your diary of everything that adds or takes away from your confidence this week.
- Rate your confidence out of 10 in the key areas of your life – for example, work, relationships, friends, family, health, finances.
- Write a page about the time in your life when you were most confident.
- Draw a graph of your confidence level over your life so far.

Increase personal satisfaction, happiness, joy or fun
- Make a note of anything fun you do this week.
- Make a note of 10 things you hate doing that you have to do regularly.
- Make a list of 20 things you have found fun in the past.
- Make a list of all the people (at least six) that you tend to do fun things with and how much time you have spent with them in the last six months.

Career
Find a new job
- Write a new résumé or get one written by a professional.
- Write a list of at least 25 of your skills and assets as an employee.
- Write a list of 20 potential contacts that could help you with your search for work.
- Write a list of 10 things you do and 10 things you don't like about your current position.

Improve my work performance
- Diarise your work tasks for the week.
- Write a job description.
- Meet with your boss to find out what he thinks of your current performance.
- List the top five areas you would like to improve.

Creative
Complete a creative project
- Define at least 20 resources you have for the project.
- Assess what stage of development you are at in your creative field.
- Make a list of your artistic accomplishments to date.
- Collate all of your artistic work so far and sort it into what you are happy with and what needs further development.

Develop my creativity
- Take note of how much time you spend on your creativity this week.
- Write a list of the creative resources you have on hand and a list of anything that is missing.
- Write 10 reasons why your creativity is important to you and 10 things that have been stopping your creativity from developing.
- Write about times in the past when you have been truly creative.

The actions I am committed to completing this week are:

1. _____

_____

_____

2. _____

_____

_____

3. _____

_____

_____

It may help to schedule these actions into your diary right now.

Bring Your Goal To Life

Imagination is more important than knowledge.

ALBERT EINSTEIN

Once you have a clear picture of where you are currently at in relation to your goal, it's time to move to the third step: 'Bring Your Goal To Life'.

I am sure you already know about the power of visualisation, and possibly already use it in some way. Visualisation is one of the mind's most effective performance tools. Athletes, musicians and performers say when they visualise their performance they are giving their mind a warm-up, in the same way they give their body one. Why not do this for your goal? By seeing your goal as already achieved, you are training your mind to believe in your goal, thus preparing your mind for the journey.

There is another thing that visualising your goal can do. I remember trying to pack my bags for a trip to the US recently. It was the end of winter here and I was heading for a hot, late summer in New York. I was having trouble knowing what to pack, because it had been cold for so long I couldn't 'see myself' in a situation where it was hot. I struggled with packing for a few hours then realised my predicament: I had to visualise the warmth to be able to prepare myself properly. For a minute or so I imagined myself wandering down a city street with a hot wind at my face. Suddenly my instincts all came flooding back – I immediately knew I would need more T-shirts, I wouldn't need any of my long warm shirts, I would need a hat for the sun, shorts for running and a towel to lie on the grass in the park. Once I could see myself in the situation it was so much easier to prepare myself for the journey.

So, visualising your goal before you even set off on your journey helps you prepare for it, by knowing what it will be like when you get there. Sometimes it might also help you get back in touch with why you really want to go. This can really help you to stay inspired week to week along what might be a challenging journey.

This next step of bringing your goal to life is more than just basic visualisation, more than just thinking your goal through. It is taking the time to imagine in detail what achieving your goal will do, what it will impact, how it will affect you. Doing this stage completely often brings surprises of its own.

Let's see what happened with my clients when they went through this process.

Melissa had spent most of her week thinking about what it would be like to have her own business. She had set herself three main actions that would help her see her goal as complete – to meet with people already in business, to research on the Internet and then to write out a vision of her life when she had her business up and running.

She had started off with organising a lunch with three self-employed colleagues, asking them what it was like compared to working for someone else. From there she surfed the Net, starting with a search for 'small business'. She ended up spending a whole evening printing out interesting articles from websites like inc.com and fastcompany.com .

The next night Melissa had asked her boyfriend not to disturb her for a while, then sat down at her desk for two hours and wrote an imaginary story of what her life would be like when she had her own business. Melissa handed me seven full pages of writing. I asked her what she had most got out of this process.

'I have never taken anything I wanted to do so seriously, normally I would probably have just gone and talked to one person, but I got so much out of this.'

'Like what?' I asked.

'Well, for a start, by talking to my girlfriends I got a lot more confident – I felt I was as good as they were. Actually I had gone to school with two of them and I used to get better marks than them sometimes, and they seemed to be doing so well. And doing the research online was good too. I could see there are a lot more resources out there than I expected – I found a site that gives you all your important forms for free, and I guess I got inspired reading about all these other small business ideas starting up. The big thing though was doing the writing. Before I did it, this whole thing sort of just made me laugh a little, a part of me was just going along with it. But now that I've written all this stuff down I have really started to believe it's going to happen.'

I acknowledged her for doing all the actions so thoroughly, and asked what else she learned from the exercise.

'I also learned there are both good and bad aspects to being self-employed. I decided that even though I have a great home office, I'd miss the camaraderie of a team a lot. So my vision included eventually working from a small, shared space with like-minded people. I also realised something pretty big – it came as quite a surprise – I wrote down that I was doing this so that I could have kids in a few years and be able to work from home. I wasn't expecting that at all, it just came out.'

'Sounds like spending a whole week focusing just on your vision has made the whole thing a lot more tangible and inevitable, rather than just a wild idea,' I suggested.

'Exactly,' she replied, smiling a little uncomfortably.

Doing this exercise had certainly helped Melissa prepare her mind for success. In the week after doing this exercise, she started noticing how many people owned their own businesses. She felt that a lot of these people had less training, contacts and 'get up and go' then she did. She also noticed an article in the paper that said over 50,000 people a year were starting businesses in her state, and mostly they were women. All this increased her confidence and thus her likelihood of success enormously.

Jan had struggled with the idea of having a relationship goal in our first session. She said she felt if someone were meant for her, then fate would just 'do its thing'. She discovered in this week's exercise that she had only dated twice in the last year, and both times with men she wasn't really interested in, 'they'd just asked me and I couldn't be bothered saying no,' she said.

The next step, visualising being in a relationship, was a bit of a turning point for Jan.

'I struggled with this,' she admitted. 'I found all these things around the house that needed doing this week. I cleaned, I tidied out my cupboards, rearranged the house even. In the end I realised what was going on and sat down and just did it.'

'I've done that myself,' I replied. 'When I was trying to write a book. The house has never been so tidy. But go on, what happened?'

'Well, I'd agreed to think about how my life would be different if I was in a relationship. So I wrote out a list of everything I could think of, then cut it down to a few main things.' Jan paused, and looked at her feet. 'I realise now that being in a relationship actually means a lot to me. I think I've been trying to pretend that it doesn't. The main things I realised is that it'd make me happier, I'd feel better about myself, I'd feel like my daughter had more of a family, and I'd feel so much better about life in general.'

I thanked Jan for her willingness to share this with me. As a coach, it is always incredibly moving to be let into people's lives and allowed to communicate on such a real level.

Performing this simple step of visualising her goal being achieved had helped Jan get in touch with the real value of achieving the goal, what it would mean to her life and to her daughter. This increased her motivation and drive to go for the goal a lot, and perhaps do things differently than she normally would.

I often find when people set a goal, their reasons for wanting to achieve it are much stronger and richer than they are consciously aware of at the time. It's almost like their unconscious is crying out to them to have something in their life, but their conscious mind is only willing to see the issue as a slight blip on their emotional radar. Bringing the goal to life allows whatever is really going on for you to come to the surface, which helps you be more honest and authentic with yourself.

Mike had done this exercise by writing out 10 things that would be different if his team got $10 million of new business in the next quarter.

> *I'd get a big bonus.*
> *We'd spend it on the new house.*
> *Other divisions would want to know how I did it.*
> *I'd get a promotion (maybe).*
> *I'd be invited to present at a board meeting.*
> *The team would get on better.*
> *The team would complain to him less about resources.*
> *The team would be happier.*
> *Everyone would be a lot busier, seeing more potential clients.*
> *I'd have to nag people less.*

I asked Mike what he learnt by doing this exercise.

'Not that much,' he replied, 'though I did get a bit more interested in going for it as a goal.'

'In what way? I asked.

'If we did even half that, I'd get a pretty fat bonus, maybe ... let me think ... hmm, probably a hundred grand or more. I hadn't realised it was quite so big. Wow. That could really help finally get this new house we've been thinking about for three years. The terrace is getting a little tight, the kids are growing up and need something bigger to run around in. Maybe this would give me the kick to get it happening.'

I asked if he felt the goal was starting to get more real for him yet.

'Well, a lot more interesting, that's for sure,' he replied.

'What about your team. There seems to be a lot about your team here, did you notice anything new?'

'Not really, I already knew they were pretty lazy. I have to push them a lot, you know. The main thing is that for us to crack $10 million it would be because a lot more of them pulled their finger out.'

It was hard not to say anything about his comments but I held myself back. It seemed to me that Mike didn't have a good rapport with his staff, and possibly there was not much respect both ways, but the only way to find out if this was the case was for Mike to see this for himself. Mike agreed to go to the next stage, to think about what was between where he was now and achieving his vision.

Action Station

Start by checking in on where you're at with your goal. Write one or two words that best capture what you are thinking/feeling about the goal at this time.

REVIEW LAST WEEK'S ACTIONS

The step-by-step nature of the coaching process requires you to assess what you learnt from the previous week in order to move forward. Therefore, there will be a section in every action station where you get the chance to look for insights from your previous week's actions.

Last week, you worked on 'Where Are You Now, Really?'. The first step is to look back and see which actions you did or did not complete out of those you committed to last week. If there are some you didn't get to, ask yourself, what was more important than getting those actions done? Did you allow work to get in the way? Did you not allocate enough time to get them done properly? It is important to see how you are prioritising your time and whether you could have done things differently so that you could complete your actions. Write down anything about this that comes to mind.

If you do not have the adequate information you need to know all about your current situation, I suggest that you transfer those incomplete actions to this week's list and make the time to get them done.

Looking at the actions you have completed, re-read what you have written. Ask yourself, what insights about yourself can you gain? What are the common themes or patterns? Imagine the work belonged to a friend. What could you learn about this person from the information in front of you?

Look back over the stories of Melissa, Jan and Mike and see what they got out of 'getting real'. Melissa realised that she is ready to start her own business and that the goal is possible. Jan realised that she had not been giving enough effort to finding the right relationship. For Mike it didn't take him long to discover which staff members were bringing in the current new business and also how much business he could expect in the next three months.

Below are some questions to ask yourself that may help you gain insights from your work.

POSSIBLE QUESTIONS TO REVIEW LAST WEEK'S ACTIONS

Finances
Save money
Get out of debt
- What have you discovered about your financial situation?
- Are you better or worse off than you thought?
- Where are you spending your money?
- What do you need to start budgeting for now?
- Are you spending more than you earn?
- How do you feel now that you have this knowledge?

Business
Start a new business
- Are the things that are missing able to be outsourced or learnt by you?
- Are you ready to start your own business now?
- Have you already done most of the legwork? If so, what else has been stopping you?
- Is your business idea viable?

Build my current business
- What are the areas that need improvement?
- What qualities do your top five clients have in common?
- What are you able to improve in your current role?
- What three things did you learn from the profit and loss statement?

Relationships
Start a new relationship
- Have you let go of the things that no longer serve you from

your past relationships?
- Are your expectations of yourself or a potential partner unreasonable?
- What are the advantages of being in a relationship?

Improve an existing relationship
- Is there a common theme to what is impacting on your relationship?
- How committed are you right now to this relationship?

Health

Increase my fitness
Increase my energy levels
Resolve a medical issue
- Did the medical give you all the information you wanted?
- Is your level of fitness better or worse than you suspected?
- Is there a common link between when you are eating unhealthy food and the environment you are in at the time?
- What is the thing that stops you giving yourself enough time to sleep/revive each day?

Personal

Decrease stress
- How much of your life is adding to your stress?
- Are the factors that decrease your stress showing up enough in your life?
- Are you honestly doing your best to look after yourself?
- What have you stopped doing now that used to decrease stress for you?

Increase confidence
- Is there a common element to the people or events that take away your confidence?
- Is there a place in your life where you are really confident?
- Has there been a time in your life when you were confident? What was different then?

Increase personal satisfaction, happiness, joy, fun
- Did you do anything fun this past week? How much of your time did it take and how long did the effects last?
- What have you stopped doing that you used to find fun?

- What is stopping you from hanging around fun people?
- What is the ratio of 'fun to not-fun' things you do every week?

Career
Find a new job
- Do you know where to look to find the job you want?
- Do you think you're qualified for your dream job?
- How close are you to being ready for your dream job?

Improve my work performance
- Are you working to your optimum?
- Was there a time when things were different at work – what has changed?
- Is improving your work performance solely up to you?
- Is there anything that you are enjoying now that you could build on?

Creative
Complete a creative project
- Do you have what you need to go ahead with the project?
- How much more do you need to make this viable?
- Do you have the right contacts to make this happen?

Develop my creativity
- Is there a theme to why your creativity is important to you?
- Was there a time when your creativity peaked in the past?
- Are the things that are stopping you easy or hard to overcome now that you look at them objectively?
- Do you have on hand what you need to express your creativity?

Try to come up with at least three separate insights.

My insights from last week's actions are:

1. _____

_____

_____

2. _____

_____

3. _____

_____

SET NEW ACTIONS

It's time to start bringing your own goal to life. There are a few great ways to do this. All of them involve thinking deeply in some way. I recommend you put aside a minimum of an hour's quiet time to do this exercise and don't let anything get in the way.

This exercise should help you prepare your mind for success, helping you to see your goal as if it was already complete, just like Melissa did. Or it might help you realise what achieving your goal would really mean to you, which is what happened to Jan. Either way, you'll find this process exciting and fulfilling in itself.

POSSIBLE ACTIONS

'Bring Your Goal To Life' is all about creating a picture for yourself of how it will feel when you have achieved the goal. To complete this step, choose one or two actions out of the following list. You can choose any that you feel most suit you and your goal, or invent your own action that you feel will work to achieve the aim of bringing your goal to life.

- Write a one-page story of what your day would be like when you achieve your goal.
- Write an imaginary story that a newspaper would run on you achieving your goal.
- Write a list of 20 things that would be different in your life when you achieve your goal.
- Write an imaginary letter to your best friend about achieving the goal.
- Do a visual collage of your life in relation to completing the goal.

Whichever one you choose, do it in as much detail as you can. If you choose to write a descriptive piece, include a perspective from all five of your senses. If your action is 'to write a list of 20 things that would be different if I achieved my goal' and you reach 20 and there are still more, then keep on writing. Give yourself the time and space to really enjoy seeing yourself achieving.

If you get stuck, stop and close your eyes and imagine yourself having achieved the goal. Read the goal over and over to yourself, aloud. This exercise is something that is best done alone and then shared with your coaching friend. When you come back to the exercise, look for elements that surprise you, like Melissa and her thoughts about children.

My actions for this week are (remember to transfer any actions you did not complete the previous week):

1. _____

_____

2. _____

_____

3. _____

_____

4. _____

_____

My vision for bringing my goal to life is:

_____

_____

What's In The Gap?

As a rule ... he who has the most information will have the greatest success in life.

BENJAMIN DISRAELI

By now you have a goal to work towards, you've seen where you are placed at the start of your journey, and you've got a sense of what completing your journey would be like. The next step is to uncover what's 'in the gap' between where you are now and achieving your goal. It's time to find out what makes your goal seem like such a challenge.

The thing in the gap might be something personal and internal, like believing in yourself enough to be able to 'just do it', or it might be something external, like leaving your current work to have time to make your new career happen. It will probably be several things.

My experience is that most of the time the answer to this question, or at least the answer that will have some value and move you significantly towards your goal, is not an obvious one. The answer tends to be something we can't see for ourselves at first.

If the answer to 'What's In The Gap?' is obvious to you already, perhaps the goal you've set for yourself is a little too easy. Also, the answer to 'What's In The Gap?' doesn't tend to be the obvious day-to-day challenges. It's not usually about having 'more time'. Even if you did have 'more time', it's quite likely it would be filled up by things other than making this goal happen.

Having a coach at this stage in the process, or getting input from someone else, can make a big difference to uncovering what's really in the gap for you. This is because human beings are great at seeing what's really going on for other people, but generally not so great at knowing what's going on for themselves.

There is an experience most of us have had that might illustrate this phenomenon a little. It's something that happens when we tackle anything new, for example, starting a new job. At first you're really excited about the job. On your first day you get up early, make sure you dress well and take care to have a good breakfast. You leave home in plenty of time to be sure you won't be late. When you first go into your new office, you're all excited. You see all the things that the job can be for you, you see its potential. You love learning about your new computer and all the great systems the company has, the business it's in, what it does. You might see a few problems in how they go about things, like the fact that your work area isn't very functional, but to you this is just something you will make better as soon as you get your hands dirty. You know what you need to do to solve any problems you see, or at the least you know will have the energy to work out the solutions as you go. It's all positive. You're seeing this new job in all its potential, without any of the resignation or cynicism that people in the next office might have.

After a while working there, maybe six months or a year, you no longer see things with a fresh mind. You no longer see the project as it could be, you see it as a long string of problems to be solved, of people getting in your way, of annoying details that stop you making a difference where you know you can.

Imagine that your life is a career. When you first became an adult, maybe as a late teenager, you felt all excited about your potential and what was ahead of you. Now an adult, you've been working on yourself as a job for so many years, you're not the same energised positive soul you used to be.

When anyone else comes along, especially someone acting as a coach or mentor, they don't see all the problems you see. They see you the same way you saw yourself years ago. It's like they are tackling you as a project for the first time. They have a fresh and clear perspective. They see you as your potential, and they can easily see what's in the gap for you to realise your goals. They see many things you can't see, and they can see that you can't see them. And they have the energy to commit to helping you get there.

This is a simple point, but one that if you grasp fully can alter the course of your life. When you live from this perspective you start to realise that in many instances you are the *least* qualified person to speak about what you are capable of! You've been 'in the job too long'. Suddenly you start listening to, and valuing, what other people have to say about you in a whole new way. My point is, take careful note of what other people might say about what's in the gap for you to realise your goals – they may be more on the ball than you think.

So what was in the gap that Melissa couldn't see, that stopped her just going out and starting her own business? She appeared to have almost everything she needed to start, and thousands of people of her age and with her skills have done it. Melissa had considered this for her homework in the last week. She came back with a list of 10 items she felt she needed to have under her belt to be able to start her business. Let's have a look at what happened.

Melissa turned up to our fourth session looking a little frazzled. It seemed as if she'd had a hard week and was battling something inside. When I asked her how she felt about her goal this week she said she'd been anxious about it for most of the week. We looked over her list of things she felt were in the gap to achieving her goals:

Feeling ready
Enough contacts
Enough money to do it how I want
A client to kick off the business with
Being old enough to be taken seriously
Great office to work from
Bookkeeper to help me
A real business plan
Knowing I can do it
The guts to just do it

I asked her what she thought of the list.

'I suppose the things in the way seem a lot smaller now, now they're on paper.' She replied. 'Stuff like finding a bookkeeper and an office and all that stuff, they're not really such a big deal. I reckon I handle much harder things than that by lunchtime most days now.'

'So what you're really saying is you can see that there's nothing really physical in the way of getting started, is that it?'

'I suppose so,' she replied.

'So what's in the gap then?'

Melissa looked from the sheet of paper in her hands to the floor. I noticed her feet swaying back and forth nervously.

'I don't know,' she replied.

'I propose you do,' I said gently, then waited silently. I could see her thinking hard while she sat there for a few seconds.

'I just don't know for sure I can do it,' she replied. Her shoulders slumped a little. 'I just don't know for sure, what if it doesn't work out?' she said, her voice going quieter.

'Melissa, is it okay if I ask you a more personal question?'

'Sure.'

'It sounds to me like you just don't have a lot of confidence in yourself, is that it?'

She let out a big sigh. 'Yeah, I guess you're right, I feel really challenged by this,' she said, looking me in the eye.

'Have you every tackled anything big in your life that you didn't know you could do for sure?'

'Well, yes, I suppose … going to uni, learning to dive, lots of stuff.'

'And what happened?'

'Well, uni was really hard, I really didn't think I'd make it through a few times, but people helped me and – ' She stopped suddenly and started laughing to herself quietly, then looked me in the eye. I saw the colour come back into her face.

'All right, I'm just not very confident in myself. That's all that's really missing. I just have to trust I can do it and give it my best.'

So Melissa had just uncovered what was in the gap for her. It was her low self-confidence and having the courage to jump in. Armed with this awareness, Melissa decided she was ready to move to the next step, to research how she could deal with her lack of confidence. She set herself an action plan to come up with 10 innovative ways of increasing her self-confidence by the next session.

What was in the gap for Jan? What was stopping her being in a great relationship? Underneath it all she was really committed to being in a relationship, she was a great 'people person', and she was fun and outgoing.

When Jan and I worked on the issue of what was in the gap for her, the results were quite surprising. It turned out she'd had a relationship with a guy called Glen that had ended four years ago. Glen had gone overseas for a job, and they'd both thought he would come back and they would continue their path together. Over time they naturally drifted apart, only speaking once a week or so. Glen had a fling that he said was nothing, but Jan had got furious and said it was over.

Jan was still mad with herself for finishing it. She still thought that one day Glen might come back and they would get together again. She realised during the session that holding on to this thought was stopping her from moving ahead. It was stopping her from being open to meeting new people. She decided to contact Glen and finish the relationship properly once and for all.

Jan phoned me during the week to share what had happened on the call.

'It was amazing,' she said excitedly. 'It feels like a huge load off my shoulders. I can see now that I was hiding behind this whole thing, as a way to avoid moving on. I'm really glad I did it, we chatted for ages, he's doing great, he isn't going to come back for years, if ever, but it still feels like I have a friend back again.

So Jan's blind spot was 'living in the past', living in hope that she would get back with Glen, instead of being pro-active about meeting people. It took great courage and faith for her to put this aside and move on, but the pay-offs came thick and fast. Jan told me the next week she suddenly noticed an abundance of interesting men in her life that she hadn't been paying any attention to.

Mike turned up for our next session a few minutes late. He looked around the room several times before he sat down. His mobile phone trilled loudly, too loud for the small room we were in. 'Just work it out, will you, I can't be disturbed,' he barked before switching it off with a huff.

'Sorry,' he said, with a calmness that seemed strained. 'Been a crazy week.'

After a few minutes of getting settled I asked Mike how he'd gone with working on what he thought was missing to achieve the goal.

'I'm not sure if I was on the right track,' he replied. 'It seemed similar to last week's thing a bit, plus I've been so busy, I only really thought about this an hour ago.

We looked over his list together.

WHAT'S MISSING TO GET TO $10 MILLION SALES
Sales team seeing more people every day
Closing more deals
Whole team working together better
People keeping to their deadlines
People being less lazy
Putting more time into presentations
Losing less people
Having more money to spend

'So do you notice a common theme in the list?' I asked.

'Time, maybe,' he said. 'We don't seem to ever have enough time.'

'Time is always a challenge,' I replied. 'What about something a little deeper, something beneath the surface? Can you see a theme here that might be common to most of what you wrote, something that if it was there, would make it much easier for you to achieve this goal?'

Mike sat and stared at the list, angling his head slightly left and then right, as if this would help him see things better.

'I'm stumped,' he replied, his jaw moving from side to side.

'There's something I can see,' I said. 'Can I tell you?'

'Oh, please do.' He settled back into his chair.

'To me what's missing is your team's motivation, and not just "rah rah" stuff, but truly motivated and excited about going to work, about achieving something together.'

'You're not wrong there,' he said, his jaw stretching forward again. 'They're mostly a bunch of no-hopers, they'd hardly lift a finger if I didn't make sure they did.'

'So do you think it would make a major difference if they were more motivated and inspired to work? Do you think if they were, you'd have a real chance of achieving this goal?'

'Well, of course. We have enough sales people to do $20 million if half of them were as productive as our top four people.'

'Then it sounds to me like that's the thing that's missing most. It sounds like you need to work out how to motivate and inspire your people. How do you feel about that?'

'Just fine, except that I've tried it God knows how many times already. I've sent them off to courses and paid for bonuses, and it's all been a waste of good money.' Mike let out a deep sigh as he said this.ƒ

'Are you willing to look into this again, to see if there are other options, more effective ways of doing this?' I asked tentatively.

'I suppose so … as long as it's not too expensive. And I'm not sending them on another training program to learn how to pass oranges between their chins again.'

I assured him it wasn't to do with orange-handling skills and we both had a good laugh, which seemed to dissolve the tension a little. We talked about how he could move to the next step, how he could research his options for getting the team motivated. Mike thought it was a good idea to talk to some friends who were doing well managing large sales teams in another industry, and ask them for a few ideas. He also decided to talk to several of his people and get a list of what his top three people did that his others didn't do. Mike seemed really happy with these actions and left the session with more of an open mind than I had expected.

One of the things you may be noticing is how systematic this whole process is. That is one of the great strengths of this system. Instead of rushing in and attacking something straight away, we take the time to uncover the deeper issues, the bigger picture, what's really going on in any area of life. We do lots of research; we make sure we are on the right track before leaping in. When we do take action, we move strongly, taking the most powerful or well-thought-out action, not just something to make things better on the surface for the short term.

At the same time, as you would have seen with the three clients in the story so far, everyone goes through their own personal journey. There is no 'right' way to be in each stage, no particular point at which everything is supposed to become clear. Some people have big insights about themselves at week 2, others at week 12. Jan discovered something that was very personal, Mike discovered something a little more external, but still an important thing that he was missing. Whatever is there in your journey will be right for you.

Action Station

WHERE ARE YOU AT WITH THE GOAL?

Write one or two words on what you are thinking about your goal right now.

_____

_____

REVIEW LAST WEEK'S ACTIONS

Look over what you created last week to bring your goal alive. Choose the key points that inspire you (this may be the whole thing) and put them somewhere you will be able to see them or read them on a daily basis. Then summarise your insights below.

My insights from last week's actions were:

1. _____

_____

2. _____

_____

3. _____

_____

SET NEW ACTIONS

POSSIBLE ACTIONS

The best way to do this exercise is to write a list. Write down all the things you can think of that are in the gap between where you are now and achieving the goal. Write them all down, no matter how silly or trivial they may seem. Try to get a list of at least 10 ideas.

LIST OF WHAT'S IN THE GAP

1. _____

2. _____

3. _____

4. _____

5. _____

6. _____

7. _____

8. _____

9. _____

10. _____

Once you have the list, put it away for a few days, come back to it with a fresh mind, or with a friend, and see what kind of patterns you notice on your list. What's really going on? Is it that you 'don't have time' or is it that you are too scared? Is it really that you 'don't have the money' or are you afraid to take a risk? Be honest with yourself, as honest as you possibly can be. Write down what is really stopping you from achieving the goal at this time. Look at Mike as an example – he thought that the gaps to his goal could be changed by having more time, whereas I was able to see that what his team really needed was to be truly motivated.

What is really stopping me from achieving the goal is:

_____

_____

_____

_____

_____

_____

_____

Research Your Options

Minds are like parachutes – they work best when open.

ANONYMOUS

I live near the beach and often take walks along the promenade for a bit of a break when I am working from home. There are showers at several spots along the promenade, used all day by a parade of surfers and swimmers. I've often been there in the mornings and watched the showers first go on, and noticed how the flow of water runs down the beach. It seems to follow the easiest path through the sand at first, going where the sand is lowest, finding its way down the beach in bits and spurts. After a few minutes the water cuts a small groove in the sand and starts to move faster, sticking to the same pathway. After a little longer the groove is quite deep, almost like a channel, and there's no way now the water will flow along any other path.

Modern neuro-science has shown that the mind works in a similar way. When you first learn to ride a bicycle, once you stop falling over so much and get a sense of how to balance, the pathways between the neurones in your brain become like those grooves in the sand. Electrical impulses have travelled the same pathway to keep you from falling over so many times, that it becomes automatic that the electrical impulses will go that way each time now. That's why if you don't ride a bike for years then pick it back up again, your brain remembers what you need to be able to balance, without having to learn it all over again. The grooves are still there.

The positive side to this is that we get to live life without having to learn things anew every time we do something we've already done. Imagine having to learn to drive again every time you hadn't driven for a few days!

The down side to all this is that once you've done something one way a few times, unless you put in some real force to change things, you will almost automatically do it the same way forever. You will do things out of 'habit'.

All of this is a big precursor to this next step, 'Research Your Options'. This step gives you the power to choose *how* you want to tackle the issues that are in the way of you realising your goals, rather than automatically doing things the way you always have. Doing this means you're likely to get a very different result from what you have in the past.

If you want to start a business but the thing in the gap for you is you're terrible with details, instead of carrying your old habit forward and 'sweeping the details under the carpet', by researching your options you could decide to partner up with someone who loved details, for instance.

Or perhaps you want to lose weight, and know the gap for you is a real lack of discipline. At this stage, instead of being tougher on yourself (the thing that most people try at first), you get to research lots of different ideas for dealing with a lack of discipline. Maybe it's something not so obvious. For example, you might find that taking up a team sport is a lot more effective at dealing with a lack of discipline than being tough on yourself. You'd have lots of other people counting on you to turn up to practice all the time, which would be a better structure for doing lots of exercise than just trying harder on your own. Not only that, you might also add some extra fun and excitement to your life, which would be a bonus in itself, and might have other spin-offs that impact on your confidence and weight.

The next session with Mike was our first by telephone. I felt like this session might be a turning point for him and took a deep breath to settle myself before I picked up the ringing phone that I knew was him. We spent a few minutes getting rid of distractions so he could focus, then started reviewing what he had learned from his actions this week.

'Mike, you're clear now that getting your team more motivated is the gap to realising your goals. And you're also clear that how you'd normally go about doing this hasn't worked in the past. So what did you discover when you looked at what your top people did that the rest didn't?'

'Lots,' he replied. 'Just about everything was different. They came to work earlier, they left later, they made more calls in a day, they saw more people, they followed up with everyone, when the others often left things hanging with people. I suppose overall they were a lot more pro-active, like calling clients that the others would never think of, and networking more on their private time.'

'What do you think is behind all that?' I asked.

'I don't know, maybe they are just more … hungry, or committed, but I'm not sure of your point. I still don't see how to make the others be more like that,' he replied.

'Mike, do I have your permission to go a little deeper on this issue with you?'

'Okay.'

'What do you think is at the base of these people being more committed?'

'I don't know, maybe they need the money more?'

'Well, maybe, that could be one of the things in their mind, but that won't help you here. What else could be behind it? What makes these people more committed?'

'I guess at the core they just want to work more,' he said, almost as a question. 'Maybe it's something more important to them?'

'Exactly!' I replied. 'It sounds to me like they really *want* to work,' I said. 'They don't just come in every day because they have to.'

Mike was quiet while he tried to process this. 'But I don't get it, how can I make people *want* to work more? I don't think that's possible, is it?'

'Mike, you've just hit the nail on the head,' I said, lowering my voice. 'It's impossible to make people want to work, in fact it's impossible to make people want to do anything, and it sounds like that's just what you've been trying.'

Mike went quiet again. 'So what do I do then?' His voice was softer now. 'If I can't make people do what I want, how do I achieve this goal?'

I suggested we look over what he got from talking to his friends, to see if there were any answers or insights in there. Mike had emailed me the list before the session.

TOP 10 THINGS THAT JOHN, MARK AND RICHARD
DO TO MOTIVATE THEIR PEOPLE
Taking the top people out on the boat each month for a big barbecue.
Giving people really big success bonuses.
Having weekly meetings offsite to set and debrief on weekly goals.
Taking one top person out to lunch each week and getting to know them.
Giving people time off for personal things.
Being more like a coach than a manager.
Taking time to listen to people when they have problems at work.
Helping people with their personal problems.
Remembering birthdays and anniversaries and giving small gifts.
Helping people set goals for themselves.

'So what do you see in this list?' I asked.

'I see lots of things that are fine for my friends to do, it's their own business, not a multinational they're working for. But for me to do most of this kind of thing … I don't know, you don't know my people, they'd walk all over me, I'd lose all my authority. And I don't see how this has anything to do with getting the team to get $10 million of new business. Maybe I could look at the bonuses and the goal setting, and maybe an offsite meeting, but the rest – '

'Mike, I need to interrupt you for a second. I feel like there's something we're really close to here and I want to stay on track.'

'Go on, then,' he said.

'This stage is about researching your options for dealing with how to motivate your people. You're clear now that what you've tried in the past hasn't worked. And you've seen that fundamentally people are motivated because they want to work. And you've realised there's no way to make them want to work. So all that's left is to create an environment where your people *naturally* want to work. Once you have people wanting to work, you can start looking at how to get the team focused solely on this goal.'

'I suppose what my friends are doing is putting a lot of effort into making sure their people love their jobs,' he said, looking at his list.

'You're absolutely right. Everything on your list is your friends attempting to create an exciting, supportive and caring environment so that their people are happy to come to work. Is that something you are willing to try?'

'I ... I ... what if they just walk all over me?' he spluttered. I could feel his pain as he tried to get his head around this new way of thinking. At 45, with 15 years of being a corporate manager behind him, the grooves in the sand were deep.

After a minute of complete silence Mike spoke up. 'Okay, let me take the week to think about this and see how it feels,' he said quietly. I thanked him for being willing to try a new idea, and we finished the session.

For Mike, researching his options was a major turning point. It allowed him to see what he really needed to do to motivate his staff, and it brought the truth home to him in a way that would change the whole course of his future. Imagine if he had decided to go straight into action once he knew the main thing was to motivate his team. The outcome may have been very different from what happened over the next few weeks.

Melissa's week had been a turning point. Midway during the week she had started writing a list of what she needed to do to increase her confidence. Halfway through the list she had a great insight – she realised she just needed to make a decision and get on with it. She picked up the phone immediately and called her boss at home and told her she was giving two weeks' notice the next day. Now she was committed.

When she put down the phone she had a sudden flurry of panic. She patched this over by spending the rest of the evening talking excitedly on the phone to three of her friends with businesses. She asked their advice on the best way to kick off her business and wrote down lots of ideas. Things like advertising, having a launch, getting an investor, meeting potential clients one on one, doing a direct mail campaign, and several versions of PR stunts that might get her name out there. At our next session we discussed all her options and she decided to do some more research into which ones would be the most likely to succeed.

Having resolved everything with her ex-boyfriend, Jan said she felt more freedom than she'd felt for years. She was ready to be in a relationship again.

We talked about what kind of plan she had for meeting new people and it became clear she'd hadn't put much thought into it yet. She decided to write a list of everything she was looking for in her 'best relationship ever', then bring that back to five main things she was looking for. Once she had her shortlist, she was going to think about 10 places she could meet this kind of person. Jan seemed a little uncomfortable about the last action but was willing to give it a go.

Action Station

Where are you at right now with the goal? Read the goal out aloud and consider how it is affecting you at this time. Make a note of it in a couple of words.

_____

_____

REVIEW LAST WEEK'S ACTIONS

Take a look at what you discovered to be the major thing(s) stopping you from reaching your goal. Read aloud what you wrote and check to be sure that you have reached the core thing that is stopping you from achieving your goal. If it rings true for you then go on to the next section. If not, go back to your list from last week and work again on finding a central theme to the things that are holding you back. Keep on working until you have the answer that you are sure is right for you.

Think about that thing that is holding you back – has it come up in other areas of your life? Is it something that only bothers you when you have to do something important? Is it something that you have overcome previously? Write down at least three insights that have come up for you in relation to 'what's in the gap'.

1. _____

2. _____

3. _____

Other: _____

SET NEW ACTIONS

This is a chance for you to totally open up to all the possibilities that will move you towards your goal. It's important at this stage that you don't just jump in and do the first thing that comes to mind. Treat your life with the respect it deserves – take the time to research all of your options properly. Too often we do what is easy or familiar rather than what is right. For Melissa, having one-to-one lunches was going to be the hardest path in some ways – she'd have to call people, make appointments and learn to sell herself, something she was very uncomfortable with. For Mike, just imagining treating his sales team better filled him with doubt, but he also agreed that it was the right thing to do.

We are now going to look at some possible actions that will close the gaps you discovered in the last chapter, and give you more information for getting to your goals.

Below are some possible actions for all goal areas that will help you research your options. Consider using these actions, or if they are not appropriate, create your own. Seeing the tone and structure of the following suggestions should help you develop your own actions.

POSSIBLE ACTIONS

Finances
Save money
Get out of debt
- Make an appointment with a financial planner.
- Read the top three finance books and list 10 tips that could work for you.
- Ask three wealthy friends for their five top tips with money.
- Check out all the other options for your personal loans/mortgage that are available right now.
- Contact all of your creditors and see what alternatives are available with your repayments.
- Write a list of 10 possibilities for increasing your income.

Business

Start a new business

- Visit your top three potential competitors and write an appraisal of their products and services, customer service, general appearance and value for money.
- Make a list of business support/start-up organisations in your area and what they offer new business. For example, funding, support, training, networking opportunities.
- Make a list of five possible investors in your business.
- Ask three business owners for their top tips on making their business work.
- Write a list of courses you could do to help your learn how to start your own business.

Build my current business

- Make a list of the top three management courses.
- Ask your top three personnel how they would improve the business.
- Read the top three marketing books and make a list of ten possible ways to improve the business.
- Phone your top three clients and ask them how they would improve your business.
- Make a list of 10 potential clients for your current business.

Relationships

Start a new relationship

- Make a list of 25 things you want in a potential partner.
- Find out how three people you know met their partners.
- Write a list of 10 places where the type of partner you want would hang out.
- Research social clubs or organisations in your local area and make a list of five that sound interesting.
- Write a list of 10 options for how you could meet a potential partner.

Improve an existing relationship

- See a relationship counsellor.
- Make a list of five relationship books that you could read together.

- Make a time to speak to your partner and assess your relationship.
- Ask five friends to list the five strengths and five weaknesses of your relationship.
- Ask three friends in great relationships to tell you their secrets of success.

Health
Increase my fitness
Increase my energy levels
Resolve a medical issue
- Check out all of the sporting clubs in your area and find out which fit into your timetable, price range and fitness level.
- Go to one dance class, yoga class and aerobics class, and assess which one you enjoy most.
- Read the top three books on improving your health and make a list of 10 options for you.
- Go to a nutritionist and/or naturopath and get five tips on improving your health.
- Surf the Net for information on your medical condition, support groups and any breakthroughs overseas. Find out the best place in the world for you to be treated.

Personal
Decrease stress
- Go see a stress therapist.
- Ask your family how they believe you could decrease stress – make a list of the top five suggestions.
- Write a list of 10 tasks you could delegate at work and at home.
- Write a list of 20 leisure activities you have only ever dreamed of doing.
- Make a list of 10 stress-reducing tips from the books in your home library.
Increase confidence
- Ask five people to list your five greatest assets.
- Ask a good friend for five things you could do to improve your confidence.

- Ask your boss to assess your work performance and make a list of the top three areas you perform best in.
- Make a list of five achievements in your future that would make you feel confident.
- Make a list of at least 25 small things you could do to boost your confidence on a daily basis.

Increase personal satisfaction, happiness, joy or fun

- Make a list of 25 activities you think would be fun to do.
- Ask three friends what they do for fun.
- Make a list of clubs in your area that sound fun to you.
- Ask the happiest person you know for their three top tips on having a great attitude.
- Make a list of 25 possible achievements that you think would satisfy you.

Career

Find a new job

- Contact three people working in your dream job and ask them how they got the job.
- Find three job agencies that deal with your dream profession.
- Speak to personnel at your current position about the possibility of moving within the company.
- Write a list of 15 ideas for getting your dream job.
- Read a top-selling career book and list five tips on how to land your dream job.

Improve my work performance

- Ask three co-workers for suggestions on how you could enjoy your work more.
- Make a list of 10 areas you think need improvement.
- Read a top-selling book on motivation and write a list of five options for improving your work.
- Make a list of 20 ways that your workday could be more enjoyable.
- Make a list of 20 things that people you admire at your work do in their jobs.

Creative
Complete a creative project
- Research the five most successful exhibitions at your favourite gallery and write a list of common attributes.
- Write a breakdown of all materials and costs involved for three different exhibition options.
- Write a wish list of personnel you would like to have involved.
- Write a list of at least five artists you could collaborate with.
- Write a list of five venues around town that you could use and the advantages and disadvantages of each.

Develop my creativity
- Write a list of 10 teachers/classes in your area.
- List 10 different ways you could apply your talent.
- Ask three creative people you know for their top tips on how they foster their creativity.
- Make a note in your diary during the week of what times you feel most creative.
- Write a list of 25 small ways you could incorporate creativity into your life every day.

I would suggest that you come up with at least four actions to research your options. Effective research takes time but it is time that will pay off when you need to determine how you will move towards your goal.

The actions I have agreed to do to research my options are:

1. _____

_____

_____

_____

2. _____

_____

_____

3. _____

_____

_____

4. _____

_____

_____

Other: _____

_____

_____

Make A Choice

In any moment of decision the best thing you can do is the right thing, the next best thing is the wrong thing, and the worst thing you can do is nothing.

THEODORE ROOSEVELT

By this point in the process you should be starting to gather momentum on your journey towards achieving your goal. You will have just completed researching your options, something that is often a powerful and expansive experience. You might be feeling as if your world has expanded suddenly, that there are so many possibilities to choose from you're not sure which way to turn.

I remember when I was first thinking about becoming a coach. At first, all I thought about was coaching people one-on-one for three months – that was my whole view of the business and what I should do. Then I decided to do some research. I started looking around and talking to other business people about my ideas. I soon realised there were lots of other ways to do what I wanted to do. I could develop a television show on coaching, run big workshops for the public, coach electronically on the Internet, deliver coaching on cassette tapes, run a coaching school, put coach training into universities, or develop coaching into a franchise. Suddenly the possibilities were endless, and almost overwhelming. How could I choose what was right for me?

You've probably had this experience yourself. You've got all these great options in front of you and you can't work out which way to turn. The options all look so good you almost don't want to have to choose. It might have been when you were deciding on a career path back in school, or deciding between two people to date, or deciding on a place for a holiday.

A lot of people freeze up at this point. They feel they can't make any decision, in case they make the wrong one. So they just stop in their tracks, not knowing which way to turn. I have been in that place many times, including when I was trying to work out what direction to go in with the coaching business. Then I realised making no decision was driving me nuts! I *had* to decide. So I worked out a process for making hard decisions that I now teach coaches to use, which I am about to give you.

There's an old nautical expression I often think of when I'm stuck in indecision: 'You can't steer a ship that's not moving.' In other words, its easier to change course once you've started, when you have momentum, than it is to try and work out the perfect answer before you start.

One of the main reasons I think this is very true is that if you can't make your mind up, generally it just means you don't have enough information yet. So rather than struggling with a decision you're not ready to make yet, go and get more information. The best way to do this? Just start in any direction that feels like a reasonable guess, just get moving, so at least you are on your way. Once you start, you'll start getting feedback from the world, and your 'automatic guidance system' kicks in and tells you if you've made the right choice or not.

There's something I can really relate to that Winston Churchill once said: 'The absence of alternatives clears the mind marvellously.' You know that feeling when you finally sit down and make a decision about something important? It's like a load lifts off your shoulders. Suddenly all your uncertainty and unresolved questions disappear. Now that you have no alternatives, the mind can easily work out what it needs to do next. It's while it has too many options that it all gets a little cloudy.

THE BIG DECISION TOOL

Over the years of my being a professional coach, one of the things I have noticed that people struggle with is making a decision. If there is something important at stake, like a career or partner choice, the struggle sometimes becomes exhausting - both for the client and for me! Sometime along the way I developed a simple system for helping people make difficult choices. I call this the Big Decision Tool, and it's designed to help you make important decisions in a very short time. One of the things that makes this tool work so well is it brings together values, emotions and logic onto the same page. The end result is you get to make a more informed choice with a higher degree of objectivity than we can normally access.

This process has two phases. The first phase involves developing clear parameters which will determine your choice; the second phase involves carefully checking your options against your parameters.

PHASE 1 – DEVELOPING CLEAR PARAMETERS

Developing clear parameters is where you get to be clear about what you're looking for from your choice. For example, if you were in high school and choosing a career, and had, say, six main choices you were thinking about, you would need to establish what your most important issues, priorities or values are in relation to your ultimate career. Does the career have to be about making lots of money, or having a lifestyle? About travel, or about getting settled? About being challenged constantly, or about not having to put too much focus on your work at all? To develop a set of parameters, you need to think these kinds of things through, and write down everything that's important to you, ending up with a list of 10 or 20 items. The next part of this first phase is to then refine or reduce that list to your top five points. Your parameters might end up being something like 'top money, lots of challenge, international opportunities, flexibility, and fun'. These are the things that are most important to you in this case. Now you have this shortlist it will be much easier to work out which of your options match this. This is where the second part of the process comes in.

PHASE 2 – CHECKING YOUR OPTIONS AGAINST
YOUR PARAMETERS

At the start of his famous book *The Road Less Travelled*, M. Scott Peck talks about how much of our energy in life is spent trying to avoid any type of risk or pain. He proposes that we are always searching for the 'path of least resistance' in life, and how this may be stunting our growth as a culture. In the second phase of the Big Decision Tool, your job is to go against the grain of normal thinking and look for the 'path of most likely success'.

What you do in this phase is create a grid where you rate all of your options against all of your parameters, giving each option a rating out of 10 for each parameter. Doing this properly takes some of the emotion out of the choice, and helps you get more of a complete and logical perspective on things.

For example, if you had five career options and five main parameters, you would draw up a chart like this on paper, or better yet, on a computer spreadsheet.

	Money	Challenge	International	Flexibility	Fun	Totals
Human resources						
Accounting						
Web design						
Veterinary						
Drama teacher						
Artist						

Once you have set up the chart, take the time to think about each option, starting with human resources, and work out how likely this area would fulfil each parameter, using a rating out of 10. So, for example, if human resources is extremely likely to give you top money you'd write in a '10', if it was only half likely, a '5'. If you're not sure exactly how each area stacks up against your parameters, go and do a little basic research. Go onto the Internet, get a book, ask a friend in this industry. Do something, read something or ask someone till you get more information that helps you get an idea of how your area looks for each parameter. Obviously you can't read the future, so there will be an element of guesswork involved.

However, if you use the same way of working through the whole chart, the process will almost always be really valuable.

Once you have completed the chart you then add the numbers up at the end and start to see which areas are your strongest, as in the following chart:

	Money	Challenge	International	Flexibility	Fun	Totals
Human resources	7	5	8	4	7	31
Accounting	7	4	4	2	3	22
Web design	8	7	9	9	6	39
Veterinary	9	7	4	3	6	31
Drama teacher	5	8	7	6	10	36
Artist	4	8	6	10	10	38

in the chart above you can now start to see that it's a race between being a Web designer and an artist. These two have the highest chance of giving you what you want overall. Sometimes people just go with the top number, other times they realise in doing this that one of the parameters is more important than others, and go with a different choice. In some ways the act of seeing the numbers on paper gets you thinking seriously about whether the choice at the top of the list is right for you.

I have done this with many clients who have found it a valuable thinking tool for their personal and professional lives. I think you'll find that once you have used this process a few times for important decisions, doing anything else just seems like guessing.

There is another simple choice exercise as old as the hills that works perfectly when you have two options: flip a coin. I know it sounds obvious, but it's actually an incredibly powerful decision tool. I don't mean that you only decide on the basis of heads or tails. The point is here that if you flip a coin seriously, you'll be able to tap into what you really feel about each option when the coin lands and you find yourself faced with that choice.

Let's see what happened when I worked with my clients to help them make the right choices for themselves.

Jan came back the next week with her handwritten list of things she wanted from her best relationship ever.

MY PERFECT GUY
Fun and easy-going
Adventurous
Attractive
Clean
Comfortable financially but not too rich
Dependable
Well-built
Cute
Laid-back
Likes the outdoors
Healthy
Funny
Good in bed
Likes a party
Not too sensitive
Has friends of his own
Same taste in music and film
Drinks a little
Doesn't smoke except when he drinks
Plays sport once in a while
Handy around the house
Single
Available

I asked her what it was like doing the list.

'It was easy,' she replied, 'and a bit of a hoot. Now I know I am serious about this again, I want to be more specific about what I want. The next one is for real'.

'And how did you go with working out your shortlist of essential qualities? What were the main themes there for you?' I asked.

'I was a little surprised when I did this. I thought it would be more about a real spunk and lots of fun, but I realised my priorities have changed a little since I thought about it last. I suppose I'm ready for something more long term now, with someone I can really count on, not just the cutest guy around. My list of five essentials was "committed, healthy, lots of fun, attractive, financially responsible".'

'Sounds like an valuable insight – good to know exactly what you're looking for before you start thinking about where to find it.'

'Oh, absolutely,' she replied, rubbing her hands together.

'So what happened with your list of 10 ways or places you could meet this kind of guy?'

'Now that was a bit harder. I asked a couple of friends and looked in a few women's magazines, I only got nine ideas.'

WHERE TO MEET HIM
Outdoor event social groups
Adventure holidays
Learning to sail
At work
Some of the good shops near work
Playing social tennis
Going to an expensive gym
Friends' parties
Up-market bars

I asked Jan if she could think of another idea now. She stopped and stared at her page for a minute, tapping her pen.

'Not really,' she replied, still looking down.

'Not really ... or "no"?' I enquired with a straight face.

'Can't get away with anything with you,' she said, only half-joking. 'There is one more, but I didn't want to write it down in case you made me do it – the Internet. I've heard of a few friends meeting new people on the Net, but it just seems so ... I don't know ... mercenary or impersonal or something.'

'Has it worked for them?'

'I'm not sure, they seem to be meeting lots of new people, I don't know if they're the right ones or not, but they do seem to be having fun with it.'

'So do you want to put it on your list? I promise I won't *make* you do anything!'

Now we had a list of 10, the next thing was for Jan to choose her options powerfully. We talked about how to do this. The key parameters for her were: the idea had to be something that could happen within the next two months, it had to be something realistic and it had to have a real chance of success. We talked about her list for a while and decided to focus on two main strategies that had the best likelihood of success, the Internet and up-market bars.

Mike turned up a few minutes early for the session and suggested we have some tea together before we started. He started telling me about his week over a steaming cup of Earl Grey.

'I'm a bit uncomfortable saying this, but I think you're right,' Mike said.
'About what?'
'This thing about making it so people want to come to work – it all started making sense this week. I talked to my wife about this, and, look, she …' He did seem really uncomfortable talking so openly, but he persisted. 'She just said she'd been trying to tell me this for years, which I suppose she has, now that I look back. She said I'm not very nice to my staff at all, and it used to upset her a lot.'
'And what do you think – is that true?' I said quietly.
'I … I … it's really hard to say this,' he struggled. 'I actually think that most of the people … think I'm a bit of a tyrant.' Mike let out a big sigh as he said this.
I was silent for a few moments and let him sit with this statement before I spoke up. 'Thanks for sharing that with me. How do you feel now?'
'Better, it was a pretty big insight to have,' he replied.
'I can see that. My guess is this is going to rock your world a little.'
'Well it already has. I sat up talking with my wife really late about all this. Then we went on to talk about our relationship and how it was all going. In the end we talked for hours and hours, more than we have in years. I was exhausted the next day, I tell you,' he added with a bit of a chuckle.

I thanked him sincerely for sharing such a personal experience, then we moved into my office to start the session formally.

We started off by working on the list of ideas that his friends worked with to motivate their people. We spent most of the session discussing the different options and creating a grid of what would really get his people loving their work more. It became clear that doing lots of them would be a great idea, but Mike decided to start with the ideas that had the highest chance of success. He decided that 'Being more like a coach than a manager' meant he would have to do many of the other things on the list, like listen better, care for them more and help them set goals. He also decided to look into setting bigger success bonuses and arranging a weekly group meeting.

When Melissa turned up to her session she was like a different person. She was brighter and happier, and even seemed taller somehow.

We went straight into discussing the options she had for getting her first three clients. She had done more work on all her options, and had a few good PR strategies for a launch of her business already. Next we devised a chart to work out the probability of success for each of her ideas and worked through this on the spot.

The winning idea was to pitch directly to people she already knew might be possible clients. Melissa squirmed in her seat when she saw that was the winner.

'What's wrong?' I asked.

'I'm not sure that's going to be so easy,' she replied. 'I have never really pitched anything before.'

'So perhaps this is the week to get organised, to start planning for success and see what you need to be great at this then. What do you think?'

Melissa hesitated then let out a sigh and agreed. She decided to look into how she was going to sell herself and how she could put together a complete presentation on her new business.

Action Station

Check on your relationship to your goal this week. Say the goal aloud to yourself and make a note of how you react to hearing it now, using a few words in the space below.

_____

_____

REVIEW LAST WEEK'S ACTIONS

Look back over what you discovered from doing your research last week and what it has taught you. Ask yourself: has your belief in your ability to achieve the goal increased? Is there something you had never considered an option for you now? Have you got less information than you had planned on?

My insights from Step 5 – 'Research Your Options' are:

_____

_____

_____

_____

SET NEW ACTIONS

It is time now to make a choice about what actions would be best from all of the options you opened up in the last chapter. The method you use to choose the action may be determined by the number of options that your research opened up.

If researching your options brought you to a small number of options that appear equally strong, you can try flipping a coin and taking note of your reaction to the outcome – that may lead you to knowing instinctively which option to take.

If you have a long list of qualities, as Jan did with the attributes she wanted in a partner, try and bring it down to five or six essential things by questioning each one individually and asking yourself whether the option is essential or just desirable. Listen to your intuition or inner voice for your true priorities.

If you have several options that you are unable to decide between, then it is time to fill in a Big Decision Tool for yourself.

The first step is to write a list of the options you have discovered across one axis of the chart. The next step is to create a list of parameters that will combine to determine which option is the best. Include everything that is important to you. For example, if you have a health goal and are trying to choose a method for getting fit, some of the parameters may be affordability, convenience, amount of equipment needed, fat burning, speed of results, muscle building, flexibility and group activity. Not all of them relate directly to getting fit, but they are all things that you know are important to question now. This is about working out how to make choices that will give you the best possible chance at achieving the goal. The next step is to reduce your list of parameters to the top five or six. Write those top parameters on the other axis of the grid. Step-by-step, you now rate each option against the parameters until the chart is filled. Add up the numbers for each option. According to what you want, the options that rated highest are your best choices for how to move towards your goal.

Now that you have made a powerful choice, it is time to set yourself some actions around bringing that choice to life. Back to the health goal for an example. If you ended up determining that jogging was the best option, it is now time to gather everything you require to start jogging right now. Your actions for this week may be 'to buy a pair of running shoes', 'to contact all the jogging clubs in my local area and find out times and prices', 'to make a list of all the local running tracks'. It is a bit like repeating the process used in 'Research Your Options' that expanded the amount of information you had to choose from, but the information is more focused now.

My actions for this week are:

1. _____
   _____
   _____

2. _____
   _____
   _____

3. _____
   _____
   _____

4. _____
   _____
   _____

5. _____
   _____
   _____

Plan For Success

He who fails to plan is planning to fail.

ANONYMOUS

You'll have noticed that we're already up to Step 7 out of 12, and we're still in the planning stages in some ways. That's one of the strengths of this system – it makes you take the time to do things properly. So far we've created our goal, we've established where we are now with this goal, we've brought it to life, and we've seen what's 'in the gap' to achieving it. We've looked closely at some options for how we can close this gap, and we've made some choices. Now we're about to do a little more planning, the last step before going out and creating major change. This next step is where we give ourselves the best possible chance of success at our chosen path. This is where we 'plan for success'.

Have you ever had the experience of wanting to do something a little challenging, and then heard a little voice inside your head say there was a real chance you could fail? Maybe you were going for a really exciting promotion at work, or you wanted to throw a big party but weren't sure if enough people would come. Or perhaps you had been serious about giving up smoking, but had already tried it several times.

There are lots of different things you could do when you hear that voice: you could pretend it's not there; you could acknowledge it, but decided to just 'think positively'; you could decide it's your intuition telling you not to do it; you could decide you shouldn't try because there's a chance you might fail. Or there is an option that seems to be the most empowering one: you could accept that your inner voice may have some validity (after all, you know yourself better than anyone else). However, in this instance, rather than have this thought stop you in any way, you could use the voice to spur you on to take the time to work out how to make your success a lot more likely.

Thinking like this requires a lot of self-honesty. It's not something everyone is comfortable with. You'll need to take a good look at issues like your resources, what new skills you might need, who you might need help from, how organised you are, even your whole attitude to your goal. Planning for success requires you to be open to new ideas, to be flexible and willing to try new things, including things that may make you feel uncomfortable at first.

For example, if you're trying to have a big party and are new to town, maybe having it with three other people is a better plan than going solo. Or if you want to give up smoking, the best plan might be to add something new to your life to take the focus off smoking rather than just going 'cold turkey'.

There are seven main issues to be aware of when planning for success. Most people tend to be good in some of these areas already but have others that could be stronger. As you read through the outlines below, you'll get a sense of which areas you are strong and weak in, and what you may need to handle to be ready for success yourself, to be running at your personal best.

1. GET SUPPORT

Most of us have a strong in-built desire to try and do everything ourselves. And if it's personal, challenging or important to us, we definitely don't want anyone's help. If this sounds a little bit like you, have a good read of this section. I propose that trying to do everything on your own will rob you of much greater success on your chosen path.

I'm going to be a little controversial here – I believe we don't work anywhere near our potential working completely on our own. I'm sure you've had the experience of trying to get an idea or project off the ground on your own, and the difference it makes when someone comes and helps you. I have had several business partnerships over the years and every time I achieved more than five times what I would have if I had gone solo. I also tried writing this book for nearly a year on my own without getting anywhere, until I finally realised I needed some help and hired a co-writer to work with me on it. Suddenly I did more in a few weeks than I had all year.

It doesn't matter if it's a friend, a partner, a business partner, a coach or a mentor, the key issue is to have someone else working on what you are working on. That's why I suggest getting a partner to work with you on this book. If you haven't got one yet, imagine where you might be up to now if you had a partner working with you every week up till now!

I think there are three main reasons why having a partner of any type is so powerful. First, instead of just thinking things through in your head you get to speak them aloud, which is a lot more powerful. Secondly, other people see things that you can't see, as they have their own set of filters and experiences. Finally, having someone else who is committed to your goal or project means you have someone else carrying the load, someone else that your project matters to, someone else driving in the same direction as you. All of this can have a major impact on your motivation levels and ultimate success.

In his book *Emotional Intelligence*, Daniel Goleman says that social isolation is about twice as risky to your health as smoking. That certainly tells me we are built to do things as part of a team, not to try to do everything on our own. People who have left the corporate world and set up home offices say one of the biggest things they miss is the social interaction – the 'water cooler moments' as some people call them. They also find they miss the momentum that comes from being around other people working on the same things. We do work better around like-minded people. What seems to be the most effective is people working in a good quiet environment without too much pressure, but with extensive social interactions and support networks available on tap.

There is another whole side to this issue of trying to do things on our own. We are actually not letting ourselves and others share in the joy of giving and receiving. We're withholding that experience. It is part of human nature to want to help others. It validates us. It's our way of letting others know we care, a way of sharing love. As James A. Autry said, 'I believe it is the nature of people to be heroes, given the chance.' Knowing we have contributed something to someone we love can be one of the most rewarding experiences in life. Yet most people don't give their friends or family a chance to contribute to them in any real way, something that would add significant value to both people's lives.

If you know that you are guilty of this kind of 'I'll do it all myself' attitude, consider the possibility that this attitude may be like wearing gumboots when you're trying to win the 100-metre dash. It just slows you down. Here are some ideas to try if you want to have a go at getting more support in your goals and in your life.

ASK FOR HELP FROM PEOPLE AROUND YOU

For some people, planning for success means learning to ask for help. Try getting in the habit of asking people around you to help you when you have an important project. I remember a coaching client of mine who wanted to meet more women, and he decided to ask his married friends for help. They loved the idea so much they organised a monthly singles party for him where three couples all brought along a single male or female. It was a roaring success. Or there was a woman who wanted to get twice as fit and asked her neighbours to help. In the end several houses in their local community all got together and started regular exercise each morning as a group, which gave everyone not just a healthier lifestyle but a richer sense of community as well. All this just by being willing to ask for help.

GET SOME PROFESSIONAL ALLIES

For you, asking for help may mean getting some allies on your team, a handful of people who have influence in your chosen field of interest. They should be people you can call on once in a while to brainstorm your ideas with, get feedback from and generally help guide you. Don't forget we are all chameleons, we all tend to unconsciously take on the characteristics of people around us. So if you spend time with people who believe in you and support your vision, you'll soon start to believe in yourself a lot more too.

FIND A MENTOR

Successful people at the end of their career often love nothing better than helping younger people starting out in the same field. Yet they rarely get the chance. Ask for help, find someone you respect and ask them to be your mentor. Arrange a monthly meeting to talk about your plans and strategies for your career. You might find rather than it being a bother for them, having you as mentor may be a tremendous gift – they get to feel they are using their life experience to make a real difference to others.

USE A PROFESSIONAL

I've seen so many people do almost anything to avoid getting professional support when it is so obvious they need it. Are you trying to do your tax on your own, when a professional could do it in 20 per cent of the time? Are you writing your own contracts when a lawyer should be doing it, which could save you a lot of money in legal costs later? Are you trying to design a logo when you have no experience at doing this, whereas if you gave your work to a designer, they would do something 10 times better in a fifth of the time? A lot of the time we need to be realistic about our limitations more than our strengths, and get the support we need to shore up the things that are not our core skills. Henry Ford is quoted as saying one of his secrets was he always hired people much smarter than him – perhaps this is something to emulate.

Getting support is all about realising you don't have all the answers and being open to other people's opinions, ideas and help. If you choose whom you ask for help wisely, getting support from others might just change your whole life.

2. GET CLEAR

Have you ever decided something and suddenly noticed new things in your world relating to your decision? Perhaps you decided to go back to school to study. Suddenly you noticed all these adult learning schools everywhere. Or you decided to buy a new house and see all these real estate magazines arriving at your house each week that you'd never noticed before.

There is a logical explanation to all this. The mind is bombarded with millions of bits of information at any time. Feelings, tastes, smells, sounds, memories, thoughts, movement. I read somewhere that people living in modern Western cities are bombarded with an average of 5000 product messages every single day. We need some kind of filter so that we are not overloaded with input, otherwise it would be hard to focus our attention on anything at all. So we tend to notice only things that are important to us right now, things that we are actually on the lookout for.

So if you want to find your dream home, you have to be clear about what your dream home is, so you can catch it when you drive past. This principle can be applied to anything we want. The clearer we are about what we want and the more it's in our conscious mind, the easier it is to find it.

For you, planning for success might mean creating a crystal-clear statement of what you are looking for, whether it's a holiday, girlfriend, new house, new career, new car or anything you're serious about attracting into your life. The clearer you are, the easier it will be for you to find what you are looking for. The best way to do this is to go through the process you have seen Melissa, Jan and Mike go through earlier – create a big list of everything, then reduce it down to a shortlist of core things that you can remember easily.

Get clear about exactly what you are looking for and success becomes a lot more likely.

3. GET ON TIME

Have you noticed that work expands to fill the time available for it? When you realise how true this statement is, you can start to use this principle to your advantage. Here are several key habits to foster if you want to start planning for success more often.

Put the important things in your life first, not the itty-bitty things. As we all have limited time, if you don't put the big things in first, only the little things seem to get done.

Set yourself deadlines for everything that's important to you. Even better, set deadlines for unimportant tasks, so they don't take all day either. Without deadlines, our tasks often seem to go on forever.

It can be really valuable to set deadlines for every meeting. If you are really challenged trying to fit all your work into each day, try setting a meeting for half the time you normally would, and see what happens.

Schedule everything in your diary. If something's not scheduled, it's not in your life. Schedule your work time, play time, relaxation time, time with your loved ones, time with your friends, time for yourself. Everything. My wife and I have a planning meeting once a week where we make sure we put in time together, time to manage our finances, time to exercise, time just hanging out together. The weeks where we don't do this for some reason have a distinctly different flavour to them – we definitely seem to have less fun and intimacy together because we haven't made sure it was in our lives.

Plan for emergencies, as emergencies happen at least 25 per cent of the time. Schedule yourself a buffer zone of time so you are always early to every important event. The difference between arriving at a meeting flustered and arriving prepared can be the difference between success and failure.

Managing your time is a vital part of living at your personal best. We all have the same amount of time, and no-one I know feels they have anywhere near enough of it. Once you accept these facts, you can start taking responsibility for managing your time to your best advantage.

4. MAKE WAY FOR SUCCESS

Planning for success might mean getting your physical environment ready for success to arrive. How you treat your physical space, your home, your car and your workspace can dramatically impact how you feel about yourself and increase your confidence and chance of success. Things like cleaning out your wardrobe of anything you haven't worn in two or three years, or cleaning out the car of all the rubbish that ends up there can leave you feeling sharp and energised. If your goal is to start a new business and your home office is a complete shambles, getting it organised may be the big thing that gets you going. Clear out your in-tray once a week so it doesn't dominate you. Clutter drains your energy, but it's so easy to get attached to it. Best to get someone to help you throw it all out. There are great books on Feng Shui and similar topics everywhere now which show you how to make the best use of your home and work spaces. Perhaps this week it's time to get stuck in, to get your environment looking the way you know it needs to.

At the back of this book, there is a personal lifestyle checklist that we use in coaching to see which areas of life people are stronger and weaker in, out of things like their health, environment, relationships, etc. If you really want to plan for success, get your life in shape by getting everything on the list at 90 per cent. Have a look at it now and do a quick rating on how well your life is balanced out.

5. BE ON THE LOOKOUT FOR SUCCESS, NOT FAILURE

Some people, no matter how well they prepare their external environment, are simply not ready for success. It doesn't happen because they can't see it. They can't see it because they are not looking for it. They are not looking for it because they are looking for something else – they are busy looking for why they won't succeed instead of why they will.

This is something that Jan learned a lot about at our next session. That week she was supposed to have gone out to three places to meet new people.

When we started our next session I asked her how she went with this.

'It was okay, I went to a new bar with a girlfriend. It was a great place, lots of cute men, but in the end it seemed like more of the same, I didn't end up meeting anyone new. I did get on the Net and found some interesting sites and checked them out, but haven't done anything about it yet.'

I sensed that Jan needed to start to be open to success instead of looking for failure, and I decided to talk this though with her.

'Jan, would you like some ideas for how you might find this kind of guy a little more easily, even how to help him find you?'

'I'm all ears,' she said, settling back into her chair.

'Great. Well, firstly I have a question. When you meet someone new that you're attracted to and think might be available, what goes through your mind? What do you think?'

'I usually check them up and down at first, see what they're wearing, if you know what I mean. Being in the trade, I can tell if they are wearing cheap or good gear. They say you can tell everything about a man by his shoes – I say it's his belt. Then I check to see if they have a wedding ring on or not, before I get too excited, then I tend to look for anything I notice that I don't like – maybe his manners, or tone, or sense of humour. I like to know what I'm in for before I get too interested.'

'So what do you do next?' I enquired.

'I don't know, I suppose if I'm in the shop and I like their look, I might flirt just a little, if they seem to be interested in me. But I don't ever really make the first move. That's a man's job. I suppose you're going to say now that's not helping, but it's just how I was brought up, you know.'

'I won't say its not helping, Jan, I'd say it's cutting your chances in half. I coach plenty of men and I can tell you, not many men are comfortable asking women out. I actually think men are more scared of rejection than women.'

'I can see how that could be true. Hmm. So really what you're saying is the only time I get to meet someone is if they like me *and* they're brave enough to flirt with me, and then I have to like them too … Sounds like a long and winding road to me, no wonder I never seem to date.'

'It's an interesting insight,' I replied.

'I suppose, well, maybe I could be a little braver, but I refuse to do a personal ad.'

'There's something a little easier that I think you'll like. It's just about your attitude and the way you perceive men.'

'What? I love men,' she said, a little surprised.

'I believe you, I promise. I want to just propose an idea here. It might not be true, but let's just see if it fits for you. Okay?'

'Sure,' she replied. 'I'm ready for something new.'

'I get the feeling from what you said earlier that when you meet someone interesting, you spend lots of energy working out all the things wrong with them. You look at them and somehow focus on all the reasons they could be wrong for you – looking to see if they have the wrong clothes, wrong look, wrong attitude, wrong physique. Does this ring true for you?'

Jan blushed a little. 'Too funny ... well, you're right ... I think I do do that, some of the time ... all right, all of the time, now I think about it. But what's wrong with that? I don't want to end up with some drop kick.'

'Let me use an analogy to explain where I'm going with this. You hire staff, don't you?'

'Of course.'

'When you interview for new people, do you suss them out and work out all the reasons they won't turn out right, or do you do something different?'

'I suppose with staff I look for the spark within them, the foundations of what I need and what I know works, like being trustworthy, you know ... good with people, committed, all that stuff, and then the rest seems to just turn out. As long as I can tell they have the basics ...' She stopped and looked up at the ceiling. 'Interesting. Maybe I can start doing the same thing, listen to men I meet almost like an interview.'

'Well, I wouldn't go that far,' I jumped in. 'They might notice. But I have an expression that defines what I mean by all this which is to "listen for the good qualities you are looking for in people, rather than for what's wrong with them". It's a great recipe for meeting more people, getting to know people better and having more opportunities for meeting the right kind of partner. In this case you could sort of listen to people to see if they have the five qualities you're looking for, instead of discounting nearly everyone up front. Most people when they do this find they meet a lot more potential partners. What do you think?'

'I think I like it a lot. I'm going to have to practise it this week and see how it goes.'

Jan decided to register for some dating sites and email some people she liked the look of, as a way to practise this new way of thinking, and to try this new way of thinking when she went out that week.

For Jan, planning for success wasn't about wearing the right dress or using a personal ad, not that I am against these things. It was about her whole approach to the subject of dating. It meant getting clear on what she was looking for, and turning that into an easy-to-remember list, then pro-actively seeking out those qualities in people. As a result she would start to focus on what she did want rather than what she didn't, which opened her eyes to all sorts of new possibilities around her.

6. GET EDUCATED

We are all capable of extraordinary things. There are people with the same brain as yours who can speak seven languages fluently, and others who play music as if they were gods. Most people, putting physical challenges aside, are capable of learning just about anything. It's just a matter of focus, time and commitment. So many times I have heard people say 'I can't do maths' or 'I can't use a computer.' It's all a matter of caring enough to take the time and get the support and resources you need. If you fell in love with someone from another country you'd probably learn the language, even if you'd never spoken a word of it in your life. We just need the incentive.

Sometimes we need to learn new skills to realise our goals. We might need to learn to speak a language, or perhaps, and more likely, it's learning how to use our current language differently to motivate others. Or we might need to learn how to write, or how to use a computer. When I started being an entrepreneur the first thing I realised was that I would need to be highly skilled at computers. At the time I had never even switched one on. I spent a year learning everything I could and at the end of the year I was completely confident that I could do everything I needed to in a way that was professional and smart. I even spent time learning how to typeset documents so they looked not just professional, but elegant and stylish. All of this was part of getting educated so that when the time came I would look the part.

Getting educated was something Melissa needed to focus on. She had some important skills to learn and needed to get skilled up quickly. When Melissa arrived for her next session she looked a little concerned. I asked her how she was feeling about her goal this week.

'The thing is, last week I was really excited about the whole thing, coming up with all these great ways of getting clients. Then during the week I realised what we'd decided – that the best way to kick it off was for me to have meetings with people. I've been so stressed since then, and I haven't done any of my actions. I never told you this, and please don't tell anyone, but I'm terrible at selling myself. I can sell anything to anyone, as long as it's not mine. What am I going to do?'

'Melissa, I said warmly, 'do you think you're unusual in not being able to sell yourself?'

'Well, I haven't thought about it, but yeah, I guess most people are okay at it, they do it all the time.'

'You might find this hard to believe, but my experience is that 99 per cent of the population are terrified of selling themselves in any way. There's something in-built that stops us being comfortable talking about ourselves, as if we all come with a button for not being comfortable at self-promoting. I don't know why we're like this, and it doesn't really matter why. What matters is not to use this fact to make yourself even less confident.'

Melissa let out a sigh. 'You're right – that's kind of funny, I guess. So what should I do then?'

'All you need to do is accept that selling yourself is challenging for everyone, and focus on getting good at it, or else outsource it.'

'Outsource it. Hmm. That's interesting. Are you saying that maybe I could get someone else to sell for me?'

'Well, you could, though you'd have to pay someone well and be sure they would be as committed as you would be.'

'That's a good point. I'm not so sure now.'

'Well, the question to ask yourself, and really listen to your gut here, is what do you think the *right* thing to do is, not the easiest thing, but the right thing?'

'I don't think anyone would ever be as committed as I would, so I'll have to do it myself. But how am I going to get good at selling myself?' she asked.

'You tell me. How do you get good at anything? Isn't it by thinking about it, talking about it, studying it, reading about it, and above all, lots of practice and preparation?'

Melissa let out a big sigh and realised she needed to get to work on her selling skills. She decided to ask a bookshop for the top three books on sales for small business and talk to a few friends already in business. Armed with this information she wanted to come up with the top 10 strategies for success in sales for small business.

For Melissa, planning for success meant giving herself everything she needed to win at the challenge she was taking on. She knew where she was going – into her own business. Now she knew how she had to do it, and next she just needed the skills to win at her chosen strategy. She needed to educate herself.

Mike had realised in the last session that he needed to get educated. Being more of a coach than manager to his team was not natural for him; he needed to undo years of one style of management and learn new ways of communicating with his staff. During the week he had gone to the Web and bought a few books on being a better manager.

'The *One-Minute Manager* really made an impact,' he said at the start of our next session. 'I loved the thing about catching people doing things right, instead of catching them doing things wrong all the time. It's so simple. It was a really easy way of remembering how to be more like a coach, and how to be nicer to people. I tried it a few times this week and I thought it went well. Though a few people looked at me a bit oddly, like they thought I wanted something, but I think they still got it.'

'That's great, congratulations on making such progress. What else did you do to get educated this week?'

'I also read *Managing to Have Fun* and got a lot from that. Mostly I got to see how not-fun work is right now.'

'So what do you want to do about that this week?'

'I hadn't thought about it yet, I guess I should really start putting in place a few ideas. Any ideas on what?'

'Maybe talking to your key people might be valuable, get them involved, see what they think, that way you have more buy-in from the whole team as they can own the ideas as their own.'

Mike decided to set up a special meeting of his five key people to discuss making changes at work, to make it more fun, and look at new ways of setting bonuses. He seemed really happy with his decision.

Getting educated had proven to be really valuable for Mike. He already had a whole bank of resources for getting educated on how to create a more supportive environment for his people. He had books, ideas, colleagues to talk to, and a team working with him on this. Next he just had to put the time in and practise being a better leader.

7. GET SERIOUS

You can tell the difference between being serious about something and not being serious about it. When you are serious about exercising, it comes first in your diary and you jog no matter what the weather is. When you are serious about managing your time at work, you learn to say 'no' to interruptions, you block your time out and get focused. When you are serious about saving money you know not to spend it on things you don't need, and you don't. Sometimes planning for success is just about getting serious – about really getting committed and making yourself your number one priority.

You might think it's selfish, but if you don't make yourself a priority, who will? If not now, when? Life doesn't ever seem to get less busy or easier. Sometimes it just takes making the leap, taking a jump into the unknown. Those who say they will be courageous when things are less scary are forgetting that courage is taking a leap into the unknown, regardless of your fear level.

STEP 7 ~ PLAN FOR SUCCESS

Action Station

Where are you at with your goal this week? Make note in a couple of words.

_____

_____

REVIEW LAST WEEK'S ACTIONS

Last week you set yourself focused actions around the best possible way of achieving your goal. What have you learnt from doing this? Have you discovered something new? Have you determined specifically how you are going to go for your goal? If so, write it down.

Also write at least three insights from getting into action on your options.

1. _____

   _____

2. _____

   _____

3. _____

   _____

SET NEW ACTIONS

Read back on how you have chosen to go for your goal. From where you are at the moment, what resources do you need to succeed at your chosen strategy? Do you need to ask for help? Would you be more likely to succeed if you were to learn new skills? Or perhaps it would help to get clearer about what you want so you can see it when it comes along? Consider what might get in the way of your success and plan ahead of time.

I have written a list of possible questions that all relate to planning for success in each goal area. Ask yourself these questions or come up with some questions of your own and write down your answers. Over the next week try to come up with a list of at least three things to include in your plan for success.

POSSIBLE QUESTIONS TO CONSIDER WHEN PLANNING FOR SUCCESS

Finances
Save money
Get out of debt
Would your financial situation be more successful if you:
- Used electronic transfers of funds to ensure that you enforce saving?
- Created an outcome for your savings – not just saving for saving's sake?
- Planned for times ahead when you are likely to blow your budget – is there another approach you can take?
- Started leaving the house without your credit card?
- Did a course on basic investing or financial planning?
- Pooled your savings with someone you know?
- Saw a financial planner?

Business

Start a new business

Would your business start more successfully if you:

- Got someone to help you with the start-up – a graphic designer to do the cards and stationery or a real estate agent to find premises?
- Did a course on self-promotion?
- Practised getting good at selling yourself?
- Approached someone to be your business partner?
- Found your first client now?

Build my current business

Would you be more likely to successfully build your current business if you:

- Shared your goal with your employees?
- Attended a course to gain extra skills? In what area specifically?
- Got more involved in all areas of the business – cashflow, promotion, and manufacturing?
- Created a new advertising campaign?

Relationships

Start a new relationship

Would it be more successful for you to:

- Be more open to meeting new people?
- Free up time for you to go on dates?
- Buy a new addition to your wardrobe or have some kind of makeover to give you a new burst of confidence?
- Practise your dating techniques on some friends?
- Start going to new places to socialise?
- Recruit a single friend to share the process with?

Improve an existing relationship

Would the likelihood of improvement be increased if you:

- Approached your partner to join you in working on the relationship?
- Blocked specific time to give to your relationship?
- Rediscovered activities that you both enjoy?
- Saw a relationship counsellor?
- Took a holiday together? A second honeymoon?

Health
Increase my fitness
Increase my energy levels
Resolve a medical issue
Would your health goal be more likely to succeed if you:
- Got a personal trainer/training buddy?
- Bought specific fitness equipment?
- Went to another country to find the best support for your medical condition?
- Enrolled in a team sport for the camaraderie and competitive nature to keep you interested?
- Changed your grocery shopping routine so that you have healthy food in the house?
- Saw a new specialist?

Personal
Decrease stress
Would you be more likely to decrease your stress if you:
- Learnt how to meditate?
- Got rid of something stressful in your life?
- Took more breaks away from your desk during the day?
- Hired a personal assistant?
- Booked in for a regular massage?
- Scheduled an annual holiday?
- Delegated more around the house?

Increase confidence
Would your confidence be more likely to increase if you:
- Did a public speaking course?
- Changed the people you interact with?
- Changed your job or work situation?
- Interacted more socially?
- Practised embarrassing yourself?

Increase personal satisfaction, happiness, joy or fun
Would your success in this area be more likely if you:
- Discovered a choice of fun places to go?
- Saw the people who make you happy more often?
- Spent more time alone?

- Started keeping a journal of the things that bring you joy?
- Scheduled fun things in your diary every week?

Career
Find a new job
Are you more likely to land your dream job if you:
- Got a consultant or agency to help you?
- Learned new interview techniques?
- Set a minimum target for the number of résumés you will send out per week?
- Told your current boss of your intention to leave?
- Allocated some money so that you can spend more time looking for your dream job instead of taking the first opportunity that comes along?
- Relocated?
- Upgraded your skills?

Improve my work performance
Would your work performance improve successfully if you:
- Recruited your boss to help you work smarter?
- Changed jobs?
- Took some time off to rejuvenate?
- Assessed whether you are doing your best right now?
- Resolved outstanding issues with any of your co-workers?

Creative
Complete a creative project
Would the project be more successful if you:
- Got an agent?
- Did a course in marketing?
- Cross-promoted with another event?
- Hired a publicist?
- Got ready for success and prepared yourself for the changes it would bring?

Develop my creativity
Would you be more creative if you:
- Cleaned out your studio?
- Made yourself a creative space?
- Made a set time to be creative?

- Spent time every week with like-minded people?
- Hired a private tutor?

As important as it is that you are as productive as possible during this coaching process, it is equally important that you don't overwhelm yourself. If you come up with a long list of things you need to ensure your success in achieving your goal, work through the list until you come up with the three most important. You can use some of the decision-making tools that you learned in 'Step 6 – Make A Choice'.

Things that are essential to my goal succeeding are:

1. _____

_____

_____

2. _____

_____

_____

3. _____

_____

_____

Actions Speak Louder Than Everything

You can't hit a home run unless you step up to the plate. You can't catch fish unless you put your line in the water. You can't reach your goals if you don't try.

KATHY SELIGMAN

Have you ever noticed that almost everything you worry about is much easier to do than you expect when you just do it? I have. Not only that, I've also noticed that worrying about doing something decreases my energy level, and doing it increases it, even if what I have to do is quite a big project. For example, I have been writing for years now, things like training courses, articles, business plans and press releases. I noticed a few years ago that every time I have something new to write, the first thing I do is worry about it intensely. I spend all this energy thinking about what I have to do, worrying and getting all anxious about whether I'll be able to come up with something good, all of which is energy that doesn't seem to do anything. Yet when I sit down and just write, with a deadline, it all comes out, I'm all excited by the end of it, and I wonder why I was so stressed in the first place!

It seems to me that thinking about taking action and taking action are two very different things. I am not saying we shouldn't think – overall I suggest we don't spend enough time thinking deeply enough. The problem seems to be we don't take enough action, which results in us thinking all the time about shallow unimportant things that we should just be doing, not thinking about.

Imagine if you never thought about things you 'ought' to be doing, such as exercising, apologising to someone you know you upset once, looking after yourself or getting your finances in order. You'd have so much more time to think about more interesting things. Like who you want to be, what your life's mission is and how you want to help others.

I have another personal rule which has served me very well. If I think about something three times, that is, if a thought that is not relevant to what I am doing at the time comes into my mind at three different intervals, then I take some kind of action to deal with the thought immediately. I may not be able to act on it completely there and then, but I do something that gets it 'off my mind'. For example, if I worry about how a new project is doing, I might write in my diary to call certain people the next day, or I do something that gets it out of my mind and into the realm of action. This one thing has changed my life and how I manage my time considerably.

When I say 'actions speak louder than everything' I really mean it. Thinking about doing something tends to do nothing. Getting in and doing it makes all the difference. Now that you have a clear goal and know how you're going to achieve them, it's time to stop procrastinating and take action. It's time for the rubber to hit the road!

Melissa turned up to the session looking pleased with herself. She showed me what she had learned about the main ideas for selling herself.

Top 10 selling skills for small businesses
Being prepared
Having meetings in the right environment
Being on time for appointments
Being comfortable with yourself
Taking time to get to know the other person
Being a good listener

Finding out what the other person needs before you tell them
what you think they need
Following up on every promise you ever make
Being flexible
Following up consistently

'I was surprised by the results,' she announced. 'I thought I would learn all about how to be "good at closing", or how to manipulate people, but I realised I'm pretty strong at most of the things on the list already. I guess there are two things to do – I need to get prepared, and I need to practise. I think if I do those two things maybe I'll be fine with the rest.'

We talked about preparation and what she needed to be able to sell.

'Remember, your goal is for you to have your first three clients within three months,' I reminded her, 'and we've got five weeks to go. What do you need to be ready, to be really prepared to start seeing potential clients?

'My goodness, I hadn't realised it was so close,' she replied. 'I need to decide on my business name, get a business card, a decent website, and do some kind of brochure on myself.'

I asked her if it was possible to complete all of that in one week.

'You're kidding, right? It takes months to do that kind of thing!' she exclaimed.

'Really? How long does it take you to think up a name and get a brochure done for a new campaign?'

'All right, I guess it's not that hard. It's just I've been thinking about a name for months, and I don't know how I could choose one in a week.'

'Can I give you some suggestions?'

'I'm all ears.'

'I propose that the important thing with a business name is that it's interesting, easy to remember and it says something about you. That it's all about first impressions. The problem is, once you've heard a name more than a few times, you're not qualified to judge if it makes a good first impression or not. So what I suggest is that you find five names that you like and are available. Then show three people you respect, and ask them to rate them in order of preference. Then choose the one that comes up with the most points. What do you think?'

'Sounds great. But how do I find out if a name is available?'

'Easy. Get on the Web, and open up four websites at once. The site for business and company names, www.asic.gov.au; the site for trademarks, aipo.gov; a site that tells you if a domain name is available, there are lots of those everywhere, a good Australian one is netregistry.com.au; and an online thesaurus, the best is thesaurus.com . It takes about 30 seconds all up to check the lot for any name, and you can use the thesaurus to inspire you for other ideas and names. It's a great way to get it done fast and effectively.'

'Sounds great, I'll have to steal that idea to help my future clients. But what about getting a website, brochure and business card done?'

'You said a few sessions ago that you did harder things before lunchtime most days ... how did you get things at work done so fast?'

'Well, I have to, we have deadlines and ...' she paused to take time to think to herself. 'Anyway, it's not just me, I get people to help me, I don't do it all.'

'Well there you go. Sounds like time to give yourself a deadline and get some help.'

Melissa laughed nervously then agreed to set herself seven days to do her name, card and a simple brochure and a website. She said she wasn't certain about the website as well but would give it a go. Sometimes all it takes to get over the big things in life is to be challenged.

I really wanted to get her going this week, now she was free of her work commitments, and this was the week in the program to be taking firm actions. I asked her what she wanted to do about preparation and practice this week.

Melissa shifted in her seat for a few seconds.

'Well, I'm so terrified I may as well practise my presentation on a friend I'm meeting for lunch and see what she says.'

'Is she the right person to practise on? Perhaps you want to do it on a few people?'

'Yeah, you're right, as soon as I said that I knew I should pick three people. I'll do one on my brother and my husband as well.'

Melissa was getting the hang of what it takes to really get results in her life. She was prepared to take action.

Mike told me in an email he had learnt a lot about the power of taking action this week. He'd picked up the phone and arranged a meeting with his key people for the next day. When they got together and he told them what it was about they were dumbfounded. They had expected to be reprimanded or told off, and instead he spent the first five minutes telling them all the things they had done right in the last 12 months as a team. Then he told them about his decision to turn the environment around at work. They didn't say much and Mike had wondered whether they were on his side yet. Then he asked them for their ideas on how to make work a better place so that people wanted to come to work. It took some time for them to warm up but after a while they got a great list together. Some of the ideas were much better than Mike had thought of himself. One was for people not to come in to work so often, that they get set up to be able to work from home one day a week.

By the time they finished the meeting they had a shortlist of five things to action as a team that week, and Mike had a whole new division unfolding before his eyes. He had never seen his people so inspired. All of this within 24 hours of deciding to take action.

Mike showed me the list of five actions at the start of our next session.

MAKING WORK FUN
Supporting people working from home one day a week
In-house drinks every Friday night
Offsite weekly meeting for 20 salespeople where we set goals and someone tells their story
Everyone gets to decorate their area how they want
Lunchtime basketball matches between the sales and admin people

I admitted the ideas were a lot more adventurous than I had expected he would go for. I asked him how he felt about the list.

'A bit anxious,' he said, 'but not too bad. The core people liked these a lot, now it's a matter of getting this out to the other 95! There are three groups of about 30-odd that report to me, on two floors, and I think I can have maybe two floor meetings to get this out to the troops.'

The Mike that set off to take action was as different to the man who walked into my office two months ago as you could ever imagine, yet he was pleased and almost excited about it all. A part of me wondered how it was all going to turn out.

Jan was bubbling over with excitement when she arrived for the next session. She'd had so much fun checking men out in this new way at work she hardly noticed she'd had the best week of sales in two years. Instead of selling her usual five to 10 suits she'd sold 18, and landed herself a $1000 sales bonus in the process. I asked her how she planned to spend the money.

'I was going to save half and blow half on a big night out. But now I think about it, maybe I should put it towards my goal a bit. I've been thinking about this new haircut for a while, and I wouldn't mind some new clothes to show off my figure a little more, I'm sure it can't hurt.'

'Sounds like a great idea,' I replied. 'You've really come such a long way since the first week, you know.'

'What do you mean?' she said.

'Well, a few weeks ago the woman in front of me was resigned and cynical about relationships, and the person here now … wow, what a difference. Now that you're listening for possibilities rather than negatives, you're like a walking, talking relationship about to happen at any instant!' Jan laughed and agreed it was a bit of a breakthrough, and decided she would spoil herself a little with this in mind.

I asked her how many opportunities she had noticed this week compared to previous weeks.

'Lots more,' she replied. 'I was delighted to notice there were a lot more men than women on all the dating websites I went to, and I found four people that seemed a lot better than I would have expected to meet there. I've sent them emails that will help me see if they have what I'm looking for. It was really easy. One of them has written back already and seems quite nice. Then, I tell you, at this new bar one night, there were two or three cute guys who I would have loved to got to know more. I chatted for a few minutes to all of them, but I didn't have the guts to ask them out on a date or anything.'

In a flash I decided this was the week for her to go all the way. 'Jan, you're so close to success now, you've come such a long way, and all you need to do is take another little jump into the unknown, do something that might seem a little scary, and you could be there, just like that. Are you willing to take the plunge and get to know three new people that interest you this week?'

'Are you kidding?' she replied. 'I haven't had three dates this year yet.'

'The thing is,' I replied, 'it will actually be easier than trying to ask just one, as you'll be much less attached to choosing the right person. I don't mean you should go on a big date or anything, you don't have to go to dinner and a movie with them. Sometimes the best dates are just getting to know people over coffee, or going for a walk with someone, going shopping with them, or even just having a quick lunch together can be great. There must be loads of opportunities like that for you. People take dates so seriously, but they should be fun and non-threatening otherwise you both either clam up or put on a false front.'

Jan liked the idea of having mini dates and eventually agreed to go for having three of them that week. Now that she was in action Jan was truly taking responsibility for what she wanted in her life.

Action Station

Where are you at with your goal this week? Make a note of how you feel about your goals this week in a couple of words below.

_____

_____

REVIEW LAST WEEK'S ACTIONS

Take a look back over what you came up with last week as essential to your plan for success. Reflect on the factors and be sure that they are the most likely ones to ensure a successful outcome. What do you notice about the elements in your plan for success? Is this the first time you will be asking for help in a long time? Have you noticed anything happening since you got clear on what you want? Are there skills you need to learn to move ahead, or are there things you need to hand over to someone who already is qualified?

My insights from Step 7 – 'Plan For Success' are:

_____

_____

_____

_____

_____

_____

SET NEW ACTIONS

This is the action station you have been waiting for. The last few weeks have been all about setting the foundation to get out there and take on some really powerful actions. This week's action station is about pushing your boundaries, getting out of your comfort zone and feeling yourself making things happen. Coaching is like anything, the more you put into it, the more you get out of it. If you have been holding back or prioritising other things while doing these actions on the side, this is your chance to make yourself number one.

Once again look back at the things you chose as essential to your plan for success. One at a time, brainstorm all the ways in which you could achieve each one. For example, if number one was to get a personal trainer, your brainstorm could look something like this:

- Ask a friend for a recommendation.
- Ask your GP for some names of personal trainers.
- Contact the local gym.
- Meet with and interview three personal trainers from the phone book.
- Phone the national fitness body for a contact list in your area.

Try doing this for all three areas.

It is likely that you have now created a huge list of possible actions for yourself. Out of that list, what are the three things that will make the most difference to achieving your goals *right now*? Not sometime in the future, but now, this week? How can you go and 'just do them'? Like Mike informing all of the staff of the new plan, or Jan asking someone out. Or Melissa setting up a meeting to practise her pitch on someone. Do the things this week that you know will make the most difference to you and your goals. I dare you!

My actions that I will complete this week are:

1. _____

   _____

   _____

2. _____

   _____

   _____

3. _____

   _____

   _____

STEP 9

Be Ready For Change

If you do not change direction, you may end up
where you are heading.

LAO-TZU

This book is designed to help you develop more successful habits in your day-to-day life, to help you be more of the person you want to be. This happens by speeding up the process of self-learning through meeting with someone committed to your personal growth every week.

Let's face it, any form of learning is generally a challenging experience. There are whole generations of adults who are uncomfortable with the idea of learning to program a video cassette recorder. Personally I find learning anything new an irritating and frustrating experience – something I do my best to avoid. It's odd when you think about it. Maybe the 'grooves' in the brain are just happier with things staying the way they are!

The truth is, learning even basic things for most people is somewhere between mildly uncomfortable and completely overwhelming. So what about going through a process where you learn things about yourself that may have a big impact on your life? Well, I'd say that's somewhere between a little confronting and completely terrifying.

It can be really useful at this point to be aware of the fact that this process can feel really challenging, and to try not to make a big deal about it. Otherwise it can be easy to let your emotions take over the show and hold you back from the real work of building better habits. The key is just to allow yourself to be challenged, but keep going regardless. Don't let it be a drama. Out of the experience of challenge, just on the other side, is often the gold that you get from the new level of self-confidence, or a key insight that comes from taking yourself beyond your normal comfort zone.

There are three things that can happen at this stage in the process. The first and most common is to resist change yourself, to fight against your own growth. The second thing that sometimes happens is you don't recognise the changes you are going through, and the third is to experience resistance from other people to your journey.

Whichever one of these you might be experiencing, this stage is about getting out of the way of your own learning process. You now have a goal worth going for, you know where you want to be and how to get there. You've spent a lot of time researching and planning, and now you've been taking action. It's time to let the whole process 'do its stuff'.

BE PREPARED FOR RESISTANCE FROM YOURSELF

It's hard to stay committed ... to stay in touch with the goal without saying there's something wrong with myself, my goal, the world.

NANCY HOGSHEAD

Sometimes when we start to take responsibility for what we say we want in life, our whole world kicks back. We find all these obstacles in the way. At times they are real things we need to pay attention to, but more often they are our old habits kicking and screaming on their way out the door. 'I'm happy with being someone who doesn't worry about how much I exercise each week, why should I change?' we say to ourselves. Change looks so hard, it looks so scary, so uncertain.

This is the point at which we have to choose. We have to choose between a future that looks just like the past or a future that we cannot yet picture for ourselves. This experience can be one of life's most challenging moments and also one of its most fulfilling. This is the opportunity to have a personal breakthrough. It's the opportunity to push past where you would normally stop and develop new habits that are more in line with who you want to be.

Melissa turned up to the session looking a little down. She sat down and stared at the floor.

'I just couldn't do it,' she said quietly.

'Couldn't do what?' I asked.

'I couldn't make a decision. I did what you said and got all the websites up at once. It was fantastic, I wish I'd known that idea months ago. I came up with five good names that I could have, I showed a few friends, but I got so many different opinions, I couldn't choose one. And now I feel stupid because I didn't do the rest of my actions, as I didn't have a name, and I think you're going to be annoyed or something. I feel like I've let you down.'

'Melissa, I promise you haven't let me down, I'm here to support you, not beat up on you. So please don't beat up on yourself, there's not much fun in that, just as there's no fun in me being tough on you, or trying to work out why you didn't do it. That's what most people do when they hit an obstacle, and none of these things will add much value to your life. If anything they stop you moving forward.'

'Okay,' she replied, 'I'll give myself a break.'

I took a deep breath then continued. 'If you're willing to be a little honest with yourself and look a little deeper, you might be able to get some great insights out of this for yourself. Most of the time when we have some kind of big breakdown in a plan in life, it's actually an opportunity to learn new things about ourselves, to have some kind of personal breakthrough. Are you willing to look closer into this and what kind of lesson there is here for you?'

'Go on,' she said. 'I'm open to looking at myself a little here. I kind of do feel like this is a turning point, a point I have to shift from.'

'So what do you feel happened inside of you that stopped you choosing a name?'

'Well, I did everything we agreed on, I got some good names, and I showed them to some people. Some liked this one and some liked that one, they weren't unanimous on any.'

'Did you show them to three people you respected and did you get them to rate the names in order of preference like we discussed?'

'Hmm. I guess I just showed them to my partner and my mum. I didn't want to bother anyone really. I just asked for their favourite name, and they both said something different.'

'I think we're getting closer to the issue here. What made you just ask your mum and partner rather than do the action properly? I know you wrote down to ask three people you respected, and get them to rate the ideas and choose the best-rating one, you read that action back to me last week.'

'I remember that too, I did write it down. It wasn't that. And the funny thing is when I went to ask my mum a part of me knew I was doing the wrong thing, I knew I was supposed to be doing it differently, but I just couldn't ...'

'Couldn't what?'

'I couldn't bring myself to ask the people I knew I had to … because … look, I knew then I'd have to go and see people and start it all up. I was just being a wus.'

'A wus,' I repeated, in the same tone as she used. I paused for five seconds then added softly, 'Is that all that's stopping you, your fear?'

'Yeah, it sounds so dumb now.'

'No, not at all, everyone gets scared. What's important is whether this is getting in the way of you achieving the results you want in your life. So the question to ask yourself is, is this something familiar for me? Does this kind of fear stop me a lot in my life?'

'Yes, there's so much I don't do because I just buckle up. I freeze up when I have to do something scary. I avoid meeting new people, I'm even shy at parties unless I drink lots. It's pretty funny when you think about it, that I want to have my own PR firm, yet I have all this fear around meeting people. Why do you think I'm like this?'

'It seems to me that most people choose an industry that gives them a chance to learn the things they really need to learn – it's very common. But I'd like to propose that we don't worry about how come you're like this. There's probably not much value in that. My question is: do you want to change? This is just a habit you have, of closing down when something scary comes along. It doesn't sound like having this habit is adding anything of value to your life, it sounds like it might be getting in the way of what you are committed to. So my question is, are you really willing to change this habit, right now?'

'How? I can't see how. It's not that easy, is it?'

'Well, it will start with the commitment and the will to change. Are you willing to change this habit?'

Melissa sighed and sat perfectly still. 'I suppose I am.'

'You suppose you are, or you are?'

'Okay, all right. It's scary you know!' she replied, her raised voice only half-joking.

'So are you ready to change this habit?' I said quietly.

'Yes, I am.'

We talked about how she was going to change. We agreed that being more conscious of when she was holding herself back out of fear would be a good first step. Melissa decided to keep a log each day of how often she didn't do something because she was too afraid. She also agreed to complete all the actions from the previous week so she was ready to start presenting her business to clients.

Melissa was right up against an old habit. She came into the series discovering the main thing holding her back was lack of self-confidence. Now she was right on the edge of doing something that would raise her self-confidence tremendously – getting her business started, and she just needed to push through and do the things that needed to be done.

RECOGNISE YOUR BREAKTHROUGHS WHEN THEY HAPPEN

Man only likes to count his troubles, but he does not count his joys.

FEODOR DOSTOYEVSKY

Sometimes doing what we think is a small action changes our whole life without us realising it. We need to be ready to catch our own breakthroughs when they happen so we can acknowledge ourselves for pushing past our normal stopping zone. This helps us build on our success. So often we don't acknowledge what we achieve, we do extraordinary things without giving ourselves the pat on the back we deserve, the acknowledgement that can give us confidence to help us over new hurdles when they come our way. It might be as simple as you decided to go running when it was cold one morning instead of sleeping in. Acknowledge yourself for this, for the willpower this took, don't just shrug it off. This will help you next time you have this challenge – you'll remember what you did last time and won't want to go backwards.

Jan had gone from three dates a year to three dates a week in less than three months. I asked her how she felt about this at our next session.

'It was a lot easier than I thought, oh, except for the first time, which was just a nightmare,' she said, rolling her eyes at the roof. 'This really cute guy came into the store for the third time this month. I wondered if maybe he was coming to see me, he seemed to be checking me out, so I thought I should ask him for a coffee. I've never asked a guy out in my life, I was so sure he could hear my heart beating it was so loud. I asked him if he wanted to grab a coffee, doing my best to pretend to be casual about it, and when he said yes I nearly passed out from the over-excitement.'

'That's fantastic! Good on you for doing this, well done for doing something that I know you were really challenged by. How did you feel afterwards?'

'Like I'd been run over by a truck. Well, at first, but after we had coffee and talked for a while I was fine. I feel a bit embarrassed actually. I thought only teenagers felt that kind of stuff, but I don't seem to have grown out of it! Anyway, he turned out to be a good guy, he's in the money market and lives near me. I think he might be back again soon, we did have a bit of a laugh.'

'So in the end it was worth going out on a limb and taking this risk then?'

'Absolutely, actually I did this a couple of times, I think I could get to like this a lot,' she said, laughing out loud.

STEP 9 ~ BE READY FOR CHANGE

'Go on,' I said encouragingly, 'I can tell you've got more to tell – what happened with your other two mini dates this week?'

'There was this guy from the Web. I can't believe I did this, but he sent me a photo, he wasn't too bad at all, and he does live in a good suburb. I know he's legit, he owns a small publishing company, I saw his photo on his website, so I invited him out for a coffee too. *Me.* Invited *him*. Can you believe it? We're meeting tomorrow. I'm a little excited, he does seem really nice.'

'Jan, that's so great, well done for jumping in with both feet. I know how hard that can be. My question is: what did you learn about yourself out of all this?'

'That if I want something, I don't have to sit around and wait for things to happen, especially with men.'

'That's a great insight, are you proud of yourself for what you did this week?'

'I guess I am a little.'

'You guess you are? That doesn't sound like someone really acknowledging herself for something as big as this. I want you to get that this is a huge change from the woman who arrived for a first session eight weeks ago. Back then you were in a holding pattern around relationships, now you're busy dating. Don't you think you could be really acknowledging yourself here in a big way, for making such a big leap?'

'It's just that I didn't get to have three dates this week as I said I would, I only had one.'

'Ah, so you're being hard on yourself here, when you should actually be celebrating. There's a saying I like – "Better to shoot for the stars, that way at least you make the tops of the trees. If you shoot for the tops of the trees you don't get off the ground." What you've done this week is shoot for three, and in going for that, you've asked two men out in one week, which is hundreds of times more than you ever have!'

Jan let out a sigh. 'I see what you mean – I'm being tough on myself when I should be celebrating,' she said, nodding her head slowly.

'Exactly. So what about a little celebration instead then?'

'How?' she replied, looking at me a little uncertainly.

'How do you celebrate anything in your life?' I asked.

'Why, a party of course, or drinks with the girls.'

'Sounds perfect to me, what do you think?'

'I think a big night out with the girls to celebrate the new me is just what the doctor ordered.'

For Jan, celebrating her change was the perfect next step to help her cement this new habit, to turn it into something that would become a natural part of her life. As well as arranging a night out, Jan decided to have another go at having three dates this week, to keep herself in the habit.

BE PREPARED FOR RESISTANCE FROM OTHERS

That's the risk you take if you change: that people you've been involved with won't like the new you. But other people who do will come along.

LISA ALTHER

I believe that gravity plays a bigger part in our lives than most of us think, but I'm talking about a different type of gravity than that of Einstein or Newton. It seems to me that each of us has something like 'emotional gravity', a force that exerts a kind of pull on others around us, just like the planets.

Think about a relationship between two people. After a while you can feel the gravity between you both holding you together. You start going to the same places, doing the same things, thinking the same ways. You orbit each other. You become like those neutron stars that revolve around each other so fast you almost can't see them as separate entities.

It's the same with any type of relationship we have, though obviously to a lesser degree. Any close relationships we have with our friends, co-workers, family or peers have some kind of emotional gravity to them.

When someone starts to grow as a person, they shoot off into a new orbit. This puts pressure on all their existing relationships. People either need to come into the new orbit with you, or the bond between you is altered in some way. Often, those other people resist moving themselves to another orbit. They may not have had the influences you had to get you to where you are now, they have just had you 'being different now'.

All this can cause rifts and friction. Either the other person has to grow too, or they try and hold you back. It's good to be aware of this process so you can look out for it happening and try and smooth things over as much as possible.

Mike turned up for our next session looking less pleased with himself than I had expected.

'So what happened?' I asked as soon as he had sat down.

'I set up two meetings, but only about half the people turned up, mostly the admin people, not the sales people I really wanted to come. I think it might be a bit of a waste of time,' he said, looking down at his feet and fidgeting.

'So what actually happened at the meeting that you did have? What did the people you speak to think about your idea of in-house drinks and lunchtime basketball and all that stuff?'

'I didn't get too far into it. I started telling people and they just seemed to stare at me blankly. So after telling them a couple of ideas I think I just said something about the management team would look into it further, and they all just kind of sat there.'

'Sounds like there might be a little cynicism in the team – is that what you found?'

'More than that, a lot of them had some pretty big objections to my first few ideas, they thought Friday drinks would be compulsory and complained about having to stay back, and some of them complained about not having space to work at home. They thought we were suggesting this to save money and space at the office. I don't know, it didn't go down so well.'

'So what do you think is happening here?' I asked.

'I don't know, I thought they were great ideas ...' he said, a little annoyed.

'Perhaps you're all gung ho and ready to make things different, but the team is still back where it was before. You might need to do something to bring it along to where you are now.'

'Sounds like exactly what's happening, but how do you think I can do that?'

'Look, I know it might sound crazy, but why don't you just ask them?' I suggested. 'Your staff are the ones most likely to know what your staff want, why not take a few out to lunch and see what's going on?'

Mike thought this was a good idea and decided to set up some informal coffee meetings with two of his people every day this week. He also decided he needed to just set up the first offsite sales meeting and make it happen. Based on his experience with the bigger group, he decided to personally call everyone on the team to let them know what he was doing and why, so he had a better chance of getting everyone's commitment.

Mike had discovered that sometimes when we change in life, others need a little time to catch up. He learned this week to make the transition as easy as possible by opening up communication channels across the board.

Action Station

Now you should be well and truly on the playing field of your own life, doing things differently, being open to new ideas, taking responsibility for what you say you want in life.

Where are you at with your goal? Say the goal aloud to yourself and write down one or two words that capture how you are feeling about it.

_____

_____

REVIEW LAST WEEK'S ACTIONS

Look back at the list of three actions that you wrote and make a note if there were any that you didn't complete. If there were, look for what insights you can gain from seeing what stopped you. Did you allow enough time to complete the actions? Had you armed yourself with enough information to get the actions done? Did you set yourself actions that were too difficult or did you let yourself get away with not doing them?

Reflect on the actions that you did do. How did it feel to take a big step towards your goal? Was it harder or easier than you expected? Make note of anything that happened differently from the way you had expected – positive or negative.

My insights and reflections from last week are:

1. _____

_____

_____

2. _____

_____

3. _____

_____

SET NEW ACTIONS

Take the above list of insights. Think about anything you went for last week that didn't work out how you expected. Make a note of anything that you can identify as either resistance from you, resistance from others or a breakthrough you had.

RECOGNISE YOUR BREAKTHROUGHS

Did you do something like Jan and overcome a fear to ask someone out on a date? Did you stick to your budget this week? Did you ask for assistance? If you had a breakthrough, it is time to really celebrate it – whatever it was that you achieved, you deserve to be rewarded. It is important though that the reward doesn't undermine the goal. For example, if you have a savings goal it would be more appropriate for you to reward yourself with cooking a special meal rather than dining out in a top restaurant and having to pay for it!

Examples of how to celebrate a breakthrough
- Go for a massage/haircut/facial/manicure.
- Buy yourself a new outfit.
- Have a night off from all the extra work you have been doing on yourself.
- Watch a show you love on TV.
- Go on a date with your partner.
- Go for a drink with your 'mates'.
- Go to a movie.
- Catch up with an old friend.
- Go for a picnic with a friend.

- Use the good crockery and cutlery, and dress in that special outfit that you never get to wear.
- Turn up your favourite music and dance around the lounge room.
- Spend a whole day by yourself.
- Drive to the country/ocean.
- Do something adventurous – abseiling, horse riding, rock climbing, surfing, go-karting.
- Buy yourself a present – get it gift-wrapped.
- Send yourself flowers at the office.
- Take a day off work and sleep in till noon.
- Cook a meal from scratch.
- Craft something out of wood.
- Open that bottle of wine you've been saving for a 'special occasion'.

RESISTANCE FROM YOURSELF

Can you see that you are your own worst enemy? Looking back on those actions, could have you gone further if you hadn't been holding yourself back or sabotaging your plan? If that's what is going on, you need to identify what is at the root of that. Is it that your confidence is low, like Melissa's? Do you think you don't deserve the goal? Whatever it is, a great way to overcome it is to create a positive affirmation in that area. For example, if the issue is that you don't think you are good enough to achieve your goal you could say 'I deserve to achieve all that I dream of' to yourself every time you feel not good enough. Make a note of how often your resistance is coming up in your everyday life. Being aware of it is the first step to being able to change it.

RESISTANCE FROM OTHERS

Without inflicting blame, was it the action of others around you that held you back in your actions? Was it your employees or your boss not supporting you? Did your partner discourage the new stuff you wanted to bring into the relationship? If the others who are holding you back are essential to your life, then you need to find a way to explain what you are doing to them and perhaps find a way to include them. If your goal is to enjoy your job more, would it help to share your career aspirations with your immediate boss? If you are trying to improve a relationship, do you need to give your partner enough information so that they can be part of the process? Whoever it involves, your best course of action here will probably be allocating time for an honest conversation with someone. You could start by telling them about your goal and then pointing out the resistance you experienced last week in getting into action. Be gentle and thoughtful – this may be hard for the other person to hear. Explain to them how they could best support you from now on.

The actions I will commit to completing this week are:

1. _____

   _____

   _____

2. _____

   _____

   _____

3. _____

   _____

   _____

Stay On The Path

*A new habit is a fragile and delicate creature that
needs to be carefully nurtured into life. The first time
it sees the light of day it is timid, cautious, and highly
impressionable. If, on entering this life, it feels
appreciated and valued, it quickly becomes a healthy
functioning entity. Should it find it has little support
or encouragement it is likely to wither and die before
your very eyes.*

DAVID ROCK

By this time in the journey, you've probably made some
fundamental changes to your life. This is the week to cement
those changes, to turn your new ways of thinking and living into
real habits. For some people this is one of the harder weeks in the
coaching journey. You might be battling to stay committed, you
may not have real evidence for the real value behind your battle,
but you also aren't willing to give up.

Just stay with it! Stay on the path to your commitments, stick
out the full journey and see what happens.

Sometimes what this takes is realising that you need new
support structures for the new you. Perhaps you need a new set of
friends who inspire you more, or you need to throw out the trashy
novels you have been reading and refresh yourself with
inspirational books and tapes to recharge your spirits daily.

Perhaps it's about asking for support from people around you, your partner, family or friends, letting them into your world a little so that they can support you in your mission. This week is about staying on the path you have spent so much time to get onto. Don't give in.

It's also a week to check with your overall strategies and make sure you haven't strayed from your intended plan too much. Or perhaps now that you've been out trying new things, you have enough feedback to readjust your plan, so that you get even closer to the centre of the path.

As you'll see from the following stories, each person's journey is different. Wherever you are at is okay, just stay with the process.

Jan turned up for our next session looking a little tired. She said her date from the Web had been postponed due to work commitments. 'Not a good sign for a first date,' she said shaking her head.

I asked her how the other ones went.

'The other guy didn't come back into the store,' she said, 'and I didn't meet anyone new this week, so all up I had a bit of a bummer of a week around this. Sales were good, and the night out with the girls was fun.' She looked up at the ceiling waiting for me to say something.

'I'm not going to give you any kind of hard time for not dating,' I said. 'That's not my job. My job is to inspire and support you in your journey towards getting your goal – a great relationship for you and your daughter. The thing is, you've really made some amazing progress in this area, and I feel that all you have to do is keep this up and your goals could be closer than you think. You're at a delicate stage, you just need to stay with it and keep going with what you know you need to do.'

'I guess you're right. I think I just got really excited about it all last week then got a bit disappointed this week. Maybe I need something to help keep this action alive?' she said.

'Could be a good idea, like maybe getting your girlfriends onto your team to be on the lookout for possible dates, maybe even get some of your staff into the game if that's appropriate at where you work. What do you think?'

'Hmm. Work could be good,' she replied. 'I'm the boss, the owner leaves it totally to me, so if I want to play around a little at work it's no problem. There's a girl who works with me on Thursday and Saturday who I could play a bit of a game with, maybe that would help remind me about staying on the lookout. She was just saying this week how I was a lot more fun as a boss since I've been in coaching …'

'Sounds like a great idea,' I replied. 'Sometimes it takes having a little support team to keep your vision alive every day. So one question I just have to ask: do you want to go for this action of having three mini dates this week? What do you think?'

'Look, I think I'm just being silly. Of course I could do that if I really focused on it. I signed onto a couple of Internet dating sites and if I spent just an hour every few days answering all those hundreds of emails I'm getting … I'm sure there's someone decent in there somewhere. Maybe I should just do it …' She paused and took a deep breath. 'Okay, I will,' she said, looking very pleased with herself.

'Excellent. Can't wait to hear what happens. The only thing that comes to mind is to make sure you don't do it for me, that you do it for you!'

'Oh, you could be right!' she gulped. 'Okay, maybe I'll look over my list once a day and read my vision I wrote early on to keep this alive.'

'Great ideas. Have a fabulous week!'

Mike told me at our next session he felt like a tug-boat trying to turn a huge stationary ship in the water, only the ship was twice as heavy as he'd expected. He assumed the big ship was his people. In truth it was his own struggle to come to terms with a new habit – being more human and real in his day-to-day life.

Mike had booked a local café for the breakfast group and sent out an email to the group of 20 but only two had responded. At first he was really disappointed and wanted to throw in the towel. Then he realised if he could just give the ship some forward momentum the steering should be easier. He steeled himself to staying on the path and decided to roll up his sleeves and make it happen.

Mike told me he had put aside two hours to talk to everyone by phone and personally invite them. In the end he found it took him a whole day to get around the group. I asked him what else he had got out of these calls.

'At first after lunch I thought I had wasted a whole day and was really annoyed by the whole thing, but after a few more hours I realised what I was doing was worthwhile. People were quite supportive one to one, a lot more than in the group. Some of them were really excited, which was great.'

'Well done for sticking to your plan in the face of unexpected challenges,' I said. 'Are there any other insights out of all this?'

'I found out why not many sales people had come to the other meeting: they expected I was going to get on their case about seeing more clients, so most of them had gone on the road. Pretty funny really. Anyway, calling everyone was great, and the other thing is I might do this once every couple of months to make sure I stay in touch with what's really going on out there.'

'Sounds like a plan to me,' I replied. 'So what happened at the meeting then?' I asked.

'About 15 people turned up, which was a really good number. More than I thought would come – word must have got around. I spent the first half telling them all about the structure of the meeting, why I wanted to do it, how it would go and all that stuff and they kind of just sat there. When we started talking about weekly goals we could set as a group, a whole lot of people actually got quite angry about it. At first I freaked out a bit and wondered what kind of monster I'd let out of the can. I tell you, you were not a popular person inside my head for a few minutes there. But then I somehow thought about what you would say in this instance, how a coach should react, and I realised I needed to just hear them out without reacting. It was so hard a few times to stop myself, but mostly I did, and it worked. They complained about a whole lot of stuff for 20 minutes, and I think they sort of expected me to just shout them down. Instead I told them to see what kind of solutions to these issues they could think of. A few people started, and after a while it all started coming together. Anyway, there are a few changes at work, we're going to change their hours and make their work more flexible so they can fit in their lives and families better. Overall it was a bit scary but actually by the end it felt really worthwhile. We decided in the end to work on the goals the next week.'

'That's a great story. I really acknowledge you for the courage it took to call the meeting and give them all the space to come forward during it. My guess is you'll soon see the rewards of this,' I said.

'I hope so,' he replied. 'It would be hard being yelled at like that every week!'

We both laughed a little and took a moment to settle down.

'So Mike, is there anything else you want to plan into your week to help you stay on the path? What about the sales themselves, how have they been going?'

'It's interesting. I have noticed the team has been seeing a lot more clients since I started paying them more attention, and we do have some hot leads on the boil now that seem to have popped up. Maybe I should take more people out for one-on-one meetings, and also check in with our sales on the computer and see how they're tracking.'

'Sounds like a good idea,' I said. 'Anything else?'

'Just something my boss said to me yesterday,' Mike replied. 'I saw him heading off to a meeting. At first he looked at me kind of funny, then he smiled and said he liked what I was up to. It was only a small thing, but it really made my day.'

We chatted for another 10 minutes about other things happening in his life. Mike said he was having a lot more fun with the kids lately. 'They said I was being more cool as a dad now,' he said and we both had a good laugh.

Melissa turned up to her next session beaming from ear to ear.

'More PR,' she said as soon as she sat down to start the session. 'It's my last name, More, and I decided to call it More PR. What do you think?'

'I love it. It's memorable, relates back to you, and has a promise in the name. Well done. How do you feel about the name?'

'Actually, I'm a bit embarrassed now. It wasn't so hard when I just sat down and did it; it took about 15 minutes on the phone. The funny thing is, one of the people I asked about the name has a Web design business. She offered to do my site for free if she could have a link at the bottom, and voila, I already have a website up, only on a free server for now, but it's up. I'm so excited!'

I congratulated her on her success. It turned out the same person designed her cards and a simple flyer during the week as well. I asked Melissa what she had learnt from this experience.

'I guess that people are willing to help, and that it pays to network with like-minded people. But that's not the exciting bit. I mean, it is exciting that I now have a business name, I registered it online, and a card and all that stuff, but what's really exciting was discovering I stop myself out of fear about 30 times a day! That's been amazing.'

'Go on', I said, 'I'd love to hear more about this.'

'Well, I had no idea. Thirty or 40 times a day! Can you believe it? It's almost like some bizarre mantra I keep saying to myself, and I had no idea it was there the whole time so much. It must be influencing me somehow, I'm sure.'

'Congratulations on getting a great insight into yourself,' I said slowly. 'And what else happened during the week? Did you notice yourself doing anything else different?'

'Well, since I've been noticing this, I've been able to catch myself about to be a wus all week. I was going to put off doing the practice runs because I was nervous, but decided to do them anyway. I did one on a friend who doesn't have her own business, and she asked me to come in and pitch to her boss who runs a business magazine. I was so excited I decided to call a few contacts I had from my old job, people who had stopped working with my agency, to see where they were at. The three people I spoke to all want to see me. One I have to call later, so all up I've got two appointments for next week. I'm so excited!'

'That's fantastic,' I replied. 'You've really come such a long way in just a few months. You're a different person now. I guess my question for you is: what can you do now to stay on this path, given how easy it is to fall backwards in life?'

'That's a good question,' she responded. 'I guess I could keep a log every day of the things I avoid doing out of fear so I can be more aware of not letting that stop me.'

'That sounds like a great idea,' I replied. 'Do you want to do that this week?'

'Sure.'

'Great, so what else could you do to make sure you stay on this new path?'

'I think it would be good to get more organised with getting new clients, like working out how many clients I want, how many people I need to see each week, and allocate different times of the week to these activities. That way I'm not just sitting around wondering what to do each day. It would be good to have some structure to follow that would give me something to focus on, so I don't freeze up as much having all this unstructured time on my hands.'

'Sounds like a great idea – do you want to do that this week?'

'Yes, it'll be great.'

'I feel like there's something else that might help, one more thing that could help keep you on track. It might be good to have an action that helps build this habit of pushing past your fears, maybe to do things differently. What do you think?'

'Mmm. I like the idea of doing things differently – how could I turn that into a real action for the week?' she asked.

'What about to do one thing every day that you wouldn't normally do. What do you think?'

'Love it. I'll let you know what happens.'

Melissa went off to research the best way to plan her week, as well as do her first presentations to potential clients. It had been a big week for her, one that she would never forget. She now had a major insight into what it was like to operate at her personal best. Like most people, for Melissa it largely came down to just getting out of her own way.

Action Station

Where are you at with your goal? Write one or two words that capture that.

_____

_____

REVIEW LAST WEEK'S ACTIONS

Last week you faced the changes that getting nearer to your goal was bringing up. Let's take a look now at the value you gained out of doing that.

CELEBRATE BREAKTHROUGHS

What did you get out of celebrating? Was it unfamiliar? Did other people notice? Do you need to celebrate more? Are there other things you have achieved that deserve celebration?

Write down three insights you gained from celebrating your breakthroughs.

1. _____

   _____

2. _____

   _____

3. _____

   _____

RESISTANCE FROM SELF

What did saying the affirmation do for you? Did it highlight for you, as with Melissa, the degree to which you hold yourself back? Did you start with one affirmation and then change it? Did you forget to even think about affirming, and if so, what does that say about the amount of care you are giving yourself?

Write down three insights you gained from dealing with resistance from yourself.

1. _____

2. _____

3. _____

RESISTANCE FROM OTHERS

If you took on this action and had that honest conversation, well done, you've just created a huge shift in your life. Think back on the conversation – what was the reaction from the other person like? Have they been able to find a better way to support you? Do you feel closer to one another? Do you feel more able to move ahead towards your goal?

Write down three insights you gained from having that conversation to diffuse the resistance you were getting from someone else.

1. _____

2. _____

3. _____

SET NEW ACTIONS

You could be in lots of places right now – maybe you have almost achieved your goal. So to stay on the path is really going to get you there. Perhaps you have been steered in another direction along the way and you need to get back to your initial direction, and perhaps new information you have gained along the way has opened up an even better path, one that you want even more.

Staying on the path is all about finding ways to support yourself on your way towards the goal. For Jan, that took maintaining the level of activity (to go on three dates per week) but to also recruit some other people into helping her to keep it fun. Mike created a new action, to phone his staff every week and to take the time to find out what was really going on for them so that he wouldn't get discouraged when they didn't respond in the way he wanted. Melissa discovered that to stay on the path to her goal, she would have to set a weekly structure for her work time herself, while also dealing with her fear. She decided to do that by taking note of when it affected her so that she had better awareness as well as facing it head on and doing something differently every day.

The first part of this action station involves you referring back to Step 3 – Bring Your Goal To Life. At that action station you wrote some kind of vision about how your life would look when you achieved your goal. Re-read the vision and ask yourself, how close to that am I now? Make notes of what you have achieved, what you haven't and anything that you have learned that is no longer relevant. Consider that you have two weeks left to achieve your goal. What is it going to take to get you squarely on the path to that goal? This is a chance for you to implement systems that will support you beyond the life of the coaching model to achieve your goal and keep on achieving.

Below are some possible actions that may help you to keep heading on strongly towards your goal.

Finances
Save money
Get out of debt

- Arrange for part of your pay to go directly to a savings account every week.
- Reduce your credit limit by half.
- Withdraw cash for spending once a week only.

Business

Start a new business

- Create a weekly structure for your time.
- Set up a support group for yourself and others you know in small business – meet once a week.
- Designate a space in your home for work only.
- Set minimum weekly targets.

Build my current business

- Set aside one hour each day for 'open door' when your staff can come and see you with any concerns.
- Take care of yourself – go home early at least one night each week and turn off your phone and home computer.
- See your boss and get a budget allocated for maintaining great staff.

Relationships

Start a new relationship

- Meet a minimum number of new people per week.
- Create a support group of singles.
- Go to a new place every two weeks.

Improve an existing relationship

- Set aside time every week to talk about the relationship.
- Book a time for a date once a month.
- Do something new together once a month.
- Set goals together for the next year.

Health

Increase my fitness

Increase my energy levels

Resolve a medical issue

- Create a reward system for yourself.
- Order groceries online to avoid temptation in the supermarket.

- Create a wall chart so that you can keep track of when you exercise; drink enough water and eat healthy food.
- Do something active every day, no matter how small.

Personal
Decrease stress
Increase confidence
Increase personal satisfaction, happiness, joy or fun
- Do something you have never done before every day.
- Spend time each evening reflecting quietly on the day.
- Attend a stress-relieving class every week.
- Recruit your friends in to finding and suggesting fun things for you to do.

Career
Find a new job
- Send at least five unsolicited applications per week.
- Phone all of your job contacts every Monday morning.
- Subscribe to industry standard publications.

Improve my work performance
- Add at least one new point to every meeting.
- Volunteer for something once per week.
- Book times to re-assess your performance with your boss four times a year.
- Do self-assessment once a month.
- Ask someone for help or delegate one task every week.

Creative
Complete a creative project
Develop my creativity
- Attend an event or exhibition that inspires you at least once a fortnight.
- Write a timetable that makes creative time the priority.
- Be active in the business side of the exhibition – attend all meetings, keep informed of all changes.
- Find a mentor in your field.

When generating actions for this week, focus on supporting yourself. How can you give yourself what you need to make the goal happen? It is not necessarily about doing more, but doing it more effectively.

My actions for this week are:

1. _____

   _____

   _____

2. _____

   _____

   _____

3. _____

   _____

   _____

Give It All You've Got

From a certain point onward there is no longer any turning back. That is the point that must be reached.

FRANZ KAFKA

This is your last week! Wherever stage you are at, this is the week to pull out all stops and go for your goal. If you've procrastinated about things that you know could change everything, this is the week to make them a priority. I have watched dozens of clients put off important actions over the years right until the last week – it's almost like they need the urgency of the deadline to get them over the line. Don't fight it, *use* the deadline, *use* the fact that this is your last week to get yourself into a zone of peak performance that is out of the ordinary. You have so much momentum from getting to this point – this is the week to hit your personal best.

> 'I got one, I got one!' Melissa shouted as she walked into my office. 'I got my first client!'
>
> 'Way to go, girl!' I yelled back. 'How do you feel?'
>
> 'So excited I can hardly stand up,' she said as she sat down.

Melissa told me the whole story. Her first meeting had been to her friend's business magazine. The presentation had gone smoothly, the boss had liked her work and loved the main point in her pitch – working with the owner of a firm and getting more attention paid to their account by a top person than they would get with a major agency. She had put in a quote in for $3000 a month and they accepted it on the spot. She'd already had a first meeting and started work.

'So what did you discover from all this?' I said.

'That it was a lot easier than I thought. I learnt that I shouldn't stop myself so much, that my ideas are good. And this thing about doing one thing every day that I normally wouldn't – wow! Can I keep doing that? That was great.'

'Of course! That one is a favourite for lots of people. So what were some of the highlights, what did you do?' I asked.

'Well, one thing was during the meeting. I was going to quote $2000 a month, I even had the price on paper, but I realised during the meeting that this was a bit low, so I just said $3000, and they didn't blink at it all. I was stunned, and of course then I wondered if I was still too cheap! But I couldn't go backwards then, it was done.'

'Congratulations and well done. What else did you decide to do differently?'

'Another day I was going to work out my schedule on just a piece of paper, but I thought maybe I should do it differently this time. I'd discovered I had proper organiser software on my computer, so I started using that to map out my week. I set up my daily schedule – one hour of new business calls first thing, then two hours of research and writing, and client meetings all between 11 and 2, then the afternoon for computer work, emailing and follow-up. I've been trying it and it seems to be working really well, it's stopped me getting overwhelmed – thanks for that idea. Oh, and the other thing was, I wrote a list of all my possible clients, and found I had about 60 people to follow up with, which was a big surprise. In my head there were only about five till I sat down and wrote the list out.'

Melissa was booming ahead now. There was little for me to do in this last week but encourage and support her to keep going to see if she could get her whole goal.

'So how did the other meetings go?' I asked.

'Oh, pretty well, I did one more pitch, which they're going to tell me about later, but that's it. I don't really have any other appointments just yet, I want to focus on this one client. I suppose you're going to say I should go for more but ...' She stopped and bit into the end of her pen for a moment.

'Rather than worrying about what I might say,' I replied, 'what did *you* say to yourself and to me, a few months ago? Isn't the goal to go for three clients? Perhaps that's why you're quiet all of a sudden?' I added, challenging her a little.

'Okay, okay, there's just nowhere to hide with you,' she said, shaking her head in mock anger.

'So are you willing to really give it all you've got and see if you can hit your target? Imagine how you'd feel if you had three.'

'That would be pretty amazing, but I'm not sure. I'm not sure I can ... oh damn it, I'm just being a wus again. All right, let's do it, I'll go for two more appointments and see what happens.'

'Is that planning for success there?'

'Urrgggh. You're right. I'll go for two more actual clients, not just two more appointments. That's at least three or four pitches. Wow. This week. I'd better get organised.'

Melissa set off to tackle her big week. She was going to go for it 100 per cent, just for the sake of it, just this week. She was going to give it her personal best.

Jan turned up to the session beaming again.

'You were right about that getting support stuff,' she said when she sat down.

'Getting my staff and friends on my team has been such a boost – though at times they've been just a little overbearing. And their taste in men sometimes leaves something to be desired. But it did really get me moving.'

I felt she had some news. I was dying to know how she had got on but didn't let on. 'So what happened?' I asked casually.

'Oh, not much, I just had five dates this week,' she said nonchalantly.

'Five! Wow, I think we've created a monster,' I said with a laugh. 'But really,' I continued, 'that's great. Any of them people you really liked, that you want to see again?'

'Actually two of them were superb. Funny thing is one of them just works around the corner from me, I've known him for years, we always chat a lot, he owns a big computer store in the centre I work in. I dropped in during the week and we got to chatting and I somehow let slip I was in coaching and working on relationships. Wow, you should have seen the conversation change at that point. Suddenly it was obvious he was as keen as mustard. We chatted for about half an hour at his shop while I was on lunch, and I asked if he'd come over to help set up a new computer at home. When he came over I'd "accidentally" cooked dinner, and he stayed a few hours and we talked over a few coffees. Nothing else happened though.'

'Ah, the plot thickens,' I said when she took a breath. 'So, do you like him?'

'I think I do, he seems like a really nice guy. He told me he thought I was seeing someone, as I never really opened up much, and that he'd always liked me. I already saw him again the other morning for breakfast before work. He called me this time, which made a nice change.'

'So have you thought about whether he is someone you'd be interested in dating more seriously? Does he fit with what you're looking for?' I asked.

'I think he does, though I haven't got to the bottom of whether he's really committed or not.'

'Sounds like something to explore this week, don't you think?'

'Good idea. Think I'll arrange a walk in the park together so we have a chance to talk more, and I want to know more about his last relationships. I've also got another guy who was really keen, someone from the Net, maybe a little too keen for me, and a bit older, but I'll go a second round there and see what happens anyway.'

I agreed it was good to keep things moving and then asked if there was anything else she wanted to do, given this was the last week of this coaching journey, to pull out all stops.

'Remember the goal is to be in the best relationship ever. What do you think?' I said.

'Maybe I just need to make this more of a priority. Hmm.' She rested her chin on her hand for a second then looked straight at me. 'Got it.'

She blurted out. 'I'm going to take three days off from work so I can focus on this area properly this week.'

I wished her the best of luck then we wrapped up the session.

Mike placed a wad of computer printouts on my desk as he sat down.

'There,' he said. 'Two more orders, it's not a breakthrough, but it is more new deals than we've had in a while.'

'Congratulations,' I replied. 'So how have the team meetings been going? More specifically, what was the second one like?'

'Really good,' he replied, raising himself in his chair a little. 'And the funny thing is, we sat down as a team and decided to set a goal of cracking $10 million of new business in the next three months. Everyone thought this was a good idea,' he said, looking a little bemused.

'Sounds like your people needed to know they were being listened to, then their natural enthusiasm was able to come out,' I replied.

'I guess that's exactly what happened. They were pretty enthusiastic this week. After we came up with this as a goal, we worked out they'd need to see an average of only one client a day consistently across the whole team and we'd easily get it. Funny, it wasn't hard. Mostly I sat back and the team worked it out. Oh, and the Friday drinks have been a big success, last week we had everyone there for the first time – over 100 people, it was big night, a lot more fun than I thought it would be. A few people's partners came too, which was great.'

'Have you asked any of the people you've been taking out for lunch what they thought about the night?' I said.

'Of course, a couple of the guys said it was a great night, they'd got to meet people they'd only spoken to on the phone before, some of whom are just one floor down in the building. And they actually said they talked a lot about work, and kind of debriefed on their week. It seemed to be really worthwhile.'

'Well, that sounds like something that'll make working on your team more satisfying, well done. I'd like to go back to your actual goal a bit for a few minutes now and spend some time on that – is that okay?'

'Sure,' he replied.

'Remember the goal is get 10 million of new sales, and so far you've realised the way to do that was to get your team really wanting to work, and you discovered you can't make them do that, that you can only create the right environment for it. For the last few weeks you've been plugging away at that, and you seem to have made some real headway there. Now that you have one week to go to complete this coaching series, I wonder how you feel about going all out for the original goal you set, *this week* – is it still a possibility?'

'Are you serious?' he replied with his brow furrowed tightly.

'Absolutely,' I said with a straight face. 'Is it something you want to really go for?'

Mike was quiet for a few moments, resting his chin against his thumb.

'That's way outside anything I've ever thought of,' he replied. 'But I guess it's possible,' he added after a moment, a tinge of excitement building in his voice.

'What would it take?' I said.

'Not that much, I'd say just closing five good-sized projects, or three big ones. We'd have about 15 in the system in process now, but usually they take forever, the admin people work on a two-week cycle to draw up offer documents, stuff like that.'

'So what would it take to make it happen this week?' I said, adding a bit of extra energy.

'Hmm. I think it would take people working five times more focused than they ever have. There's no way they'd do that though, unless there was some ridiculously huge bonus in it for them.'

'How huge?' I said with a smile.

'Whoa,' he said, sitting up in his chair, 'you're getting a little over-excited there. I was only joking about the bonus.'

'Really? How big is your bonus on cracking $10 million in a quarter – 100,000 or so?' I asked, leaning forward to get closer to him. Mike edged back from the table and sat upright in his chair. 'A little more than that,' he replied cagily.

'So what if you gave the team half your bonus, split between the people who get the deals, if they can get the target in one week? What do you think?'

'That would cost me 50 grand, are you kidding?' he said, a little flabbergasted.

'Well, are you sure it would cost you 50? What if they really did it, wouldn't you then put up the same bonus each quarter, and maybe get your division up to $40 million instead of just 10? What kind of bonus would you get then?'

Mike was quiet except for his mind ticking over loudly. He sat still, breathing heavily, for one whole minute. When he spoke, his voice was calmer. 'You might just be right,' he said, narrowing his eyes a little. 'Maybe I do just need to give away a bit more, I did say we'd review how we'd pay bonuses, and I guess I've been avoiding the whole issue. I was thinking more like doubling them, not multiplying by 20. But I do see your point …'

'I did notice it hadn't come up yet. 'So what do you think?' I asked with a smile.

'Well,' Mike replied, taking a big breath. 'Why not? I'm going to give it everything and see what happens. Let's do it.'

I told Mike if he needed to check in with me for ideas or support during the week to let me know. He left the session charged up and excited. It was going to be an exciting week in his office.

Action Station

Where are you at with your goal this week? Make a note in one or two words.

_____

_____

REVIEW LAST WEEK'S ACTIONS

Last week was about taking the time to ensure that you were giving yourself what you needed to move directly towards the goal. Take a look back at what you chose to employ as support structures. Are you now back on track for the goal? Have you increased your confidence? Do you feel as if you are supporting yourself to get there?

Write down three insights about what you learned from Step 10 – Stay On The Path

1. _____

_____

2. _____

_____

3. _____

_____

SET NEW ACTIONS

Look at your goal. Say it to yourself – *shout* it to yourself. Then state the goal as if you had achieved it. For example, if the goal is to double your income, practise saying the amount of your new income.

Make a note below of how saying that makes you feel.

_____

_____

Wherever you are right now and whatever you are feeling is okay because there has never been a better time to take great action than right now. Maybe you feel as if the goal isn't going to happen or maybe it is a foregone conclusion. Either way, this is your chance to make that goal yours. This really is it. You have come this far, spending time laying the groundwork for amazing achievements. What can you do this week to really give it all you've got? What will it take for this goal to be your priority?

Grab your diary and look at any other commitments you have this week – can you put them off for one more week? Can you delegate some of your tasks to someone else?

Here are some other suggestions for how you could give it all you've got:

- Go for twice as much as you have been – double your targets or the time you have been committing to your actions.
- Say 'no' to everything else – take time off work or go away from home and spend time by yourself. Unplug the TV, switch off the phone. What is it going to take to make the goal happen?
- Make the big decisions today. If you have been procrastinating about starting something that is essential to your goal, go and do it this week. There is no more time to think about it.
- If you don't ask, you don't get. If you are trying to start an investment, can you get a pay rise or ask someone for the cash? If you are looking for a relationship, who can you ask out?
- Do something daily. Don't let a day go by between now and next week without committing time and energy to getting this goal.

You have put in so much time up to now so give yourself the time you deserve this week to get over the line. Include any actions that you were meant to do earlier in the process that are still essential to the goal happening.

The actions I am committing to doing in my final week of coaching are:

1. _____

_____

_____

2. _____

_____

_____

3. _____

_____

_____

4. _____

_____

_____

5. _____

_____

_____

STEP 12

Celebrate Your Journey

Too many people miss the silver lining because they're expecting gold.

MAURICE SETTER

I'm going to say something a little radical now: *your goal is not the most important thing about this whole journey.*

'What!' I hear you say. 'We've just spent the last 12 weeks getting completely focused on it. How can it not be the most important thing?'

Let me say it again. Your goal is not the most important thing about this journey – it is only a tool for digging up the gold in yourself. While goals are useful, they themselves are not the gold, just the tools.

Having observed hundreds of people going through this process, I know how easy it is for people to forget this fact. Of course we get attached to whether the goals are achieved or not. It's only human. And if you're not careful, it can be easy to use not reaching a goal as an excuse to beat up on yourself. That's certainly not the point of the journey. Not surprisingly, it's not just the client that gets attached to the outcome of the goals. Often it's the coach too. It's all too easy to wrap up our self-esteem in the success or otherwise of our journey.

The real gold is not the goal you have achieved. It is the journey you have undertaken in going for the goal, and who you have become now as a result. In order to really see the truth of this, you need to change gears a little, you need to slow down. It's like what happens after taking a long journey. You can't see what the journey has meant to you until you get back home, unpack your bags and sit down to a nice cup of tea. It's then that you realise the person who left on the journey only ever drank coffee.

So this last step has quite a different flavour to all the others. It is all about putting the goals 'to bed', finishing them, wrapping them up. It's about seeing what did and didn't happen along your journey, celebrating your successes, noticing your challenges, discovering any big insights about yourself with the whole of the journey in mind. And above all, acknowledging who you have become now, compared to when you started your journey.

'What a mammoth week,' Mike said as we started our final session together. 'If I compare this to a few months ago it's like I'm in another world.'

Mike spent the next 10 minutes explaining his breakthrough week. By Tuesday not much had happened, despite telling his top eight people there was $20,000 for the person who brought in an 'A' class client that week. By Wednesday he realised he was going to have to do something radical if he was going to get any new business at all. So he did something he hadn't done in seven years. He went down to the sales room and sat with six of the phone team and started making calls with them. They were pretty shocked at first, then they listened in on his pitch and started to learn from him. Mike spent the whole afternoon working the phones, making calls himself then coaching each person on how to do better calls. By the end of the day, with six of them working on it, they had 16 appointments for the next two days, the number they normally have in a month. And the funny thing is he'd had a lot of fun.

On Thursday and Friday he went on the road with two of his top people to help get them going. Between them all, they got to 13 out of the 16 meetings in the two days, a record number ever for his division for a fortnight. They did get some new deals: $3 million worth, from a medium-sized hardware distributor needing a whole new computer system after a fire. Fortunately the company had been in a bigger hurry than Mike. The back-of-house team had worked through the night to get the contract out and by Friday afternoon it was signed and sent back.

I was a little lost for words by the end of his story. Lots of clients have major breakthroughs like this one at the end of their journey, and I often struggle to find words that honour the significance of their experience.

'I really congratulate you on such an amazing journey this week. How do you feel now?' I asked.

'I don't think I have words for it,' he replied. 'I am a mixture of many things. On the one hand I'm really frustrated and annoyed that we didn't get to the goal, on the other hand I think I'm more inspired about my work than I've been since my first day on the job.'

I suggested we go through the whole journey chronologically to get a more holistic picture of everything and see what came out of it. Mike remembered where he was at the beginning and was almost a little embarrassed by some of the things he'd said then. I reminded him of the previous three months, starting off with setting a goal that was bigger than he had ever considered going for. Then realising his team was performing under their overall potential and seeing he needed to learn how to motivate them better. Then discovering he couldn't make them work harder, that he had to create an environment in which they wanted to produce. Then came the big realisation – that he wasn't very nice to his people, that mostly they thought he was a tyrant, and realising he needed to be more of a coach. Then coming up with some good initiatives to make this happen, like catching people doing things right instead of wrong, having the Friday parties and the weekly meetings. Then struggling to get the team to align with his initiatives. Then he had taken it on himself to make his initiatives happen no matter what, then rolling up his sleeves and getting on the front line with his people to make it happen. And finally getting some fantastic new results from the group.

'I can see the whole journey a lot more clearly now,' he said as I finished. 'But I'm still a little disappointed with the result.'

'Mike, maybe we should do a bit of a reality check here. What are your new sales now, for these three months?'

'Uuhh, I guess it's 5 million, plus we have about – ' he paused and counted a few things in his head – 'about 22 pitches under way. Hmm. That's a quite a few.'

'Given you said they were on 2 million at the start, isn't that two and a half times your previously expected business in three months? Could you imagine when you started that you would have done that in three months?'

'No, no way,' he replied.

'So don't you think it might be worth celebrating your success a little here? I know it's not the full goal, but it's still pretty huge don't you think?'

I could see Mike struggling with this. After what felt like a minute his face lightened up and he started nodding to himself.

'Okay, maybe I have to look on the positive, instead of what didn't happen.'

'Exactly,' I replied. 'We've shot for the stars, but hit the tops of the trees. So what? Imagine if we'd set a goal of getting sales to 5 million, you probably wouldn't have gone all out and learned so much about yourself. So let's celebrate what you've achieved,' I added, raising my voice.

'I can see your point,' he said. 'It has been worth going for the big goal, I think I'm just being tough on myself.'

'Exactly. So can you celebrate your success a bit now?'

'Yes,' he said, letting out a deep sigh. 'Yes, I think I will.'

We spent a few minutes noting down five things to celebrate in his journey, then moved on.

'So what are the big things you've learned about yourself out of this whole journey?' I asked quietly. Mike sighed again then smiled a little uncomfortably. Even after three months of coaching, he still struggled against looking inside himself, against being in touch with his emotional journey. But he had certainly come miles from where he had started.

'I don't know … maybe I'm more aware of myself now, more real or something,' he said slowly, looking out the window.

'Can I tell you tell what I see?' Mike was still looking out the window and nodded in reply. 'I see someone who has learned to look inside himself a little more, to blame the world for his lot a bit less, and, most of all, someone who has become a lot more human. And what's more,' I continued, 'someone who is having a lot more fun living this way, and someone who won't be able to go backwards now without a part of him knowing he is ripping himself off.'

Mike looked back at me. There was a calmness in his face I'd never seen before. His eyes had softened and opened a little. I let him sit for a few minutes with his emotions, both of us savouring the moment.

We spent a few more minutes wrapping everything up and getting clear on all the insights he had gained about himself. Then we spent a few minutes thanking each other for everything. And thus Mike's journey was complete.

EPILOGUE TO MIKE'S STORY

I never know how a coaching series is going to turn out. Even after hundreds of them, they are always full of surprises. The only thing I know for sure is that believing in people and holding them to their vision makes a huge difference. What unfolds from there is always their own personal journey. Mike started out as a tough cynical client. His company was paying for part of his coaching, so he didn't have as much 'buy-in' as some of the other clients here. Along the way he discovered things about himself that may have been obvious to you and I at the start, but there was no way he could be told these things at that point. He needed to go through a journey of self-discovery. As he did, his whole world started to come to life. By the end of the journey, Mike had discovered things about himself and about his capacities that would stay with him forever. He had truly developed new habits, habits that would help him achieve his personal best for years after his coaching had completed.

Melissa had emailed me her results for the week before she turned up, so I knew what to expect. She had gone full out and seen 12 potential new clients during the week. What I didn't know was whether she'd achieved her goal or not. 'So how did you go?' I asked, trying to hide any nervousness. I knew she had really given it her all, and hoped she'd had some kind of response.

'Well, I didn't hit the goal,' she said, looking at me straight-faced. She had an odd look, something wasn't right. 'I didn't hit my goal, because I went way past it!' she yelled out, almost jumping up and down with excitement. 'I just got another four clients!'

'Oh, congratulations!' I bellowed. A big smile crossed my face. It took her a few minutes to be able to settle down enough to talk about it at all. Eventually I asked her to tell me what had happened.

'Well, I almost don't want to tell you this, but it wasn't that hard, really. I just had to realise that nothing else was worth thinking about this week except for calling everyone I could think of, making appointments and seeing them. I put everything else off, and I'm really glad I did.'

'Excellent. Sounds like you've discovered the power of having a single focus. What else did you find out this week?' I said.

'Well, I found out it wasn't that hard to call people, once I'd done a few anyway. Like I'd planned, I blocked out time each morning to do it, and called everyone on my list of 60, then made another list of 100 and went for that too. I only got through to, like, a quarter of the people I phoned, everyone's so busy, and I kept having to call back all the time. In the end most of the people I could get through to were happy with their PR, but I just kept going. I put my goal up in big letters on my wall, and I read my vision out a couple of times when I got low.'

'Sounds like you're really getting clearer about how to stay motivated and disciplined,' I said. 'Well done.'

'I surprised myself actually,' she replied. 'By Wednesday, after talking to about 80 people, I had 11 people willing to see me. I thought that wasn't great at the time, but I just kept going. I managed to see eight of them in the last two and a half days of the week.'

'Fantastic. Seems like you really gave it all you've got. So what happened at the meetings? How did your pitches go?'

'I seem to be a lot more comfortable with them now, which is great – I'm really getting my pitch down. And I'm finding I love meeting all these new people and hearing their stories, they're all so interesting, and I get so excited helping people launch new ideas,' she said.

'Congratulations,' I said. 'Sounds like this week's been a major turning point for your whole future. I think you now have a good idea of what it takes to be disciplined. It's something you'll never forget.' Melissa agreed and we talked for a few minutes about the new clients and the kind of projects each one involved. Then it was time to start wrapping up the whole series.

I started retracing her journey step-by-step to help us both get the series into perspective.

'At the start you were working 70 hours a week for $28,000 a year, working on big projects but getting no recognition. You were someone who wanted to start your own business but felt like you were years away from being ready.'

'That's right,' she said. 'Seems such a long time ago, it's great to bring that back into perspective.'

I continued. 'Then in the next few weeks you discovered just how many resources you already had, and got more in touch with why you wanted to do this – to be more in control of your life, especially for when kids come might along.'

Melissa was nodding her head and smiling. 'That really got me motivated,' she added, 'it gave me much more of a reason to do this.'

I went on. 'Then when you looked into what was in the gap, you saw how many other people your age and with less experience had their own business, and it became clear that it was mainly just a lack of self-confidence holding you back.'

'That was a real turning point for me,' she said, sitting forward in her chair.

'I think it was,' I replied. 'I remember how in that week you were going to research how to get more confident but realised you just needed to just go out and start. That was a big thing because next thing you know, you gave notice at work, and decided to kick off your business by having one-to-one meetings.'

'That's right,' she said, 'but I got a bit freaked out then about having to sell myself.'

'Yes, although once you realised this was just a new skill to learn, you got prepared, got all the materials you needed, learnt to ask for help, and practised your pitch on others.'

'That was another huge turning point-week for me,' she said. 'I chose my name and logo, got my website up and did a brochure, all in one week. That was *huge*!' she exclaimed, rolling her eyes. 'That was stuff I had been worried about for months, and I did it in a couple of days.'

'Amazing to see what you can do when you really go for it, isn't it?' I replied.

She smiled and nodded. 'Once you had everything ready, you went and did your first pitch and landed your first client,' I continued. 'Then you got really focused and totally went for it in the last week and now you have a total of five contracts. So, in summary, you've gone from someone dreaming about having your own business to having your first five clients in just three months. How do you feel?'

She seemed to be adding a few things up on paper. After a moment she looked at me, a little startled. 'I feel like I'm going to need some help,' she said. 'That's $20,000 worth of contracts lasting around four months,' she said. 'That's nearly what I was making in a year already.' Melissa laughed and shook her head again in disbelief. She wasn't expecting to achieve anything like that in her first month in her new career.

'So, is there a big insight for you out of this whole journey?' I asked once we'd both settled down.

'Lots of them,' she replied. 'Mostly about what I am capable of. I think the big thing is that I've learned I can do anything I set my mind to, which is such a great feeling. I really feel like I have a solid foundation to build this thing from now. Though of course I have no idea how it's all going to turn out, and no idea how to run the details of a business yet, but I know I can just learn it as I go along if I don't let lack of confidence stop me. The funny thing is, I still don't feel that confident, though I thought I would by now. It's just that now I'm okay to keep on moving ahead even though I'm not completely confident. I guess that's the difference.'

'Sounds to me like you've discovered the true meaning of courage: taking steps in the direction of your dreams without knowing for sure how the journey will unfold. Congratulations.'

We spent a few more minutes summing up everything she had learned from the journey, and then thanked each other for a great three months.

'It's been a great journey,' she said, 'one that I won't forget for a long time. Here, this is for you. Thanks for everything.' And with that she reached into her bag and pulled out a bottle of French champagne.

EPILOGUE TO MELISSA'S STORY

Melissa had all the highs and lows of someone throwing themselves into any big personal challenge. In this case it was the challenge of leaving the security of the corporate world and setting up her own business. The insights she discovered about herself and her capacity for courage and learning would profoundly alter the course of her future. Melissa contacted me a year or so after this coaching series to tell me some big news. She was pregnant, but fortunately had three staff managing her business so she was set up to take time out. She had grown her business from nothing to a serious small business in 12 months. 'I've never forgotten that thing about catching myself when I'm being a wus,' she said. 'There was no way I could go back to being small again without hearing your voice over my shoulder.'

That's something a lot of people find with coaching – the new habits are ingrained and truly make a difference to the ongoing quality of your day-to-day life.

Jan turned up for her last session late in the afternoon in a bright red summer dress, looking like she was ready for a party. She sat down and told me all about her week. She'd had a big walk in the park with the guy from near her work. This gave her the chance to really get to know him better. It turned out he had an ex-wife and two kids, and was having a lot of personal struggles.

'That shortlist of what I want in a relationship was really valuable,' she said. 'It kept me very focused on what I need from a relationship, rather than just falling headlong into whatever comes along. When I looked at the list after my walk with this guy, I realised how important having someone fun and easy-going was for me. I just felt like that wasn't one of his strong points. So I called him up this week and let him know I wanted to stay just friends. He was a bit thrown at first, he's had a bit of a rough trot lately, but I'm sure he'll be fine.'

'Sounds like you're really getting better at staying focused on what's important to you. That list could have saved you both a lot of heartache down the track,' I said.

She agreed with me then continued with her news. She'd also met with three guys from the Internet, and one of them turned out to be fabulous.

'He was the first one that emailed me, the one with his own business,' she said. 'He was a lot better in real life. And really cute too. We met in a café and had such a great laugh over how we met on the Net. We both expected each other to have three heads, it was hysterical! We ended up having such a good time at coffee, we spent the rest of the day together, just kind of hanging out, going shopping, having lunch on the harbour, all that kind of stuff, which I could only do because I'd especially taken time off from work. Oh, I tell you, it was the best day out I've had in years.'

'Sounds like playing full out has really paid dividends for you,' I said. 'Do you think you're going to see him again?'

'Uuhh, well, actually I've seen him three nights this week, and tonight we're going out with some friends of his.'

'Wow! How do you feel about how fast it's going, are you okay with that?' I asked delicately.

'Well, it's all going really fast, but I looked over my list a few days ago, and he's up there with all the things I wanted. Only thing is, he's a bit more good-looking and outgoing than anyone I normally go out with, but hey, no-one's perfect. Maybe he'll even keep me in line a little!' she said laughing out loud.

We spent a few minutes talking about her other dates and what had happened, 'mostly mini disasters', she said, then we settled down to review the whole of the coaching journey. Jan decided the highlights were accepting she really wanted a partner, putting the past behind her by contacting her ex, and then getting really focused on her shortlist. 'I've never got what I wanted to clear in my head,' she said. 'It really made a difference. Also the thing about focusing on what was right rather than wrong was a big issue. I really got to see why I hadn't been dating. I just wasn't going out and making it happen.'

We talked about what she had learned out of the whole process. Jan said she wasn't the same person as three months ago.

'Can you be more specific about what's changed?' I asked. 'It could be great to know exactly what you're celebrating here.'

'There's so much, I don't know where to start,' she replied. 'Overall I'm having a lot more fun than I've had in years, life seems a lot more positive than ever.'

'Why do you think that is?' I asked.

Jan looked out the window at what was now a lovely summer's day. 'Maybe I just got off my butt and started going for what I want, rather than complaining about it not happening all the time. I also think I started to lighten up a bit too. Just having someone to talk to each week, someone else really there for me, really made a big difference. That's been one of the big things.'

'Well,' I said, 'I really congratulate you for such a great journey, and want to thank you for being open to trying new things, for being so coachable. I know it's been a great journey for you, and I want you to know that I have got lots out of it too.'

Suddenly there was a beep outside the window. Jan glanced at her watch. 'Oh, I forgot to ask,' she said quickly. 'I need to finish a few minutes early today. Is there anything else we need to cover?'

'No, I think we're about done,' I replied. 'Just don't forget to stay in touch and let me know how it all pans out with this guy,' I added.

'Of course,' she said, as she started to pack up her things. I took the opportunity to sneak a look outside my window. I noticed a nice-looking guy in a BMW parked on the pavement. 'You'd better get going,' I said. But she was already halfway out the door, a grin from ear to ear. 'Thanks so much for everything, really,' she said. And in a flash of red she was gone.

EPILOGUE TO JAN'S STORY

Jan made some giant leaps in just three months. She was eminently coachable, someone ready and willing for change in her life. From the moment she put the past behind her she was ready to fly. All I had to do was keep reminding her to flap her wings and steer her in the right direction. Jan emailed me a few months after our series ended with news that things hadn't quite worked out with the guy she'd met, but she'd met someone else quickly and was now madly in love. Though the coaching hadn't got her to her goal there and then, it had helped her build the muscles to go for what she wanted in the long term. As Jan discovered for herself, coaching is not so much about achieving your goals as it is about who we become along the way.

Action Station

This week's action station is about acknowledging how far you have come in this journey, how much you have risked or sacrificed, and what new things have been revealed to you about yourself or your goal. Going over everything you have done could take up to one and a half hours so allow yourself plenty of time. Also, no matter where you are at with your goal, I'm certain that you have moved ahead. This is not intended to be a chance for you to beat up on yourself about what you could've done more of. If you are able, I would suggest scheduling this process on a day where you have little or no other commitments and when you have finished, take yourself out and do something indulgent – you deserve it.

Where are you at with the goal now? Make a note in one or two words:

_____

REVIEW LAST WEEK'S ACTIONS

What did you do to play full out and what did you get out of doing that? Did you get further than you ever thought possible like Melissa? Did you do something unexpected like Mike working with his staff rather than above them? Did you have the time to really get what you wanted like Jan? What did you put on hold? How do you feel now about the decisions you made?

Write at least three insights on what you got out of playing full out:

1. _____

_____

_____

2. _____

_____

_____

3. _____

_____

_____

THIS WEEK'S ACTIONS

1. REVIEW YOUR JOURNEY

The focus for this week is that you feel complete about your entire coaching journey. The best way to do that is to remind yourself of what you have done over the last 12 weeks and to honestly assess how the process has affected you. Go back to the start of this book and review all that you have done chronologically over the last 12 weeks. Look at the way your relationship to the goal changed during the entire process – and at how you pushed ahead regardless. Read through all of your action stations and take note of all the actions you did or didn't complete. Go through all of your insights and see if there are common themes that you learnt about yourself throughout the journey. If you are working with a partner, you could hand them your workbook and have them read to you what you did each week and what you got out of completing the actions. Make a note of anything that stands out as either an amazing achievement or something you still are not happy about. Looking back you may feel embarrassed, like Mike, by your attitude at the start of this journey. Or maybe you can see that the reason you have come so far is simply because you started doing something about what you wanted, like Jan. Whatever reaction you have, it is important that you write it all down so that you can move ahead clearly after this session.

My insights/feelings/thoughts from my coaching are:

_____

_____

_____

_____

_____

_____

_____

_____

_____

2. CELEBRATE YOUR WINS

Look at the list of amazing achievements you have written down in the exercise above. Have you given yourself credit for all that you have done over the last 90 days? Remember to look for the little wins along the way, like Mike having a great Friday night drinks party with all the staff, or Jan getting people at her work to help her look for potential dates, or Melissa coming up with a great business name. Think about what you have done and consider in what other areas in your life it will move you forward.

Say aloud to yourself or your partner how you feel about yourself right now. Are you proud? Moved? Satisfied? The happiest you have ever been? Maybe you feel something different for each thing you have done that was out of your comfort zone. That's okay, go through each one and acknowledge yourself for putting in the effort when it counted.

The things I need to celebrate from my coaching series are:

_____

_____

_____

_____

_____

3. WHAT ISSUES OR CONCERNS DO YOU NEED TO PUT TO BED?

As important as it is to celebrate what went right for you, it is equally important to acknowledge the parts that didn't go to plan. Have a look at the actions you didn't complete – is there something you can learn from this? Did you always prioritise something else instead of your goal? Did you expect too much of yourself and set too many actions? Like Mike at the start of his final session, are you unhappy with the final result? Write down all of your concerns about where you are at with the goal now.

_____

_____

_____

_____

_____

Now look at that list and say to yourself that you are willing to learn from these things and then let them go.

4. WHERE ARE YOU NOW IN RELATION TO YOUR GOAL, EXACTLY?

It's time to be objective. Look at the initial goal you set and try to give yourself a score out of 10 for where you are at right now. It could be like Melissa and be more than a 10 or it could be like Mike – a low score until you work out what it is you have actually gained. Look at the score you gave yourself and write one or two lines on what that score indicates to you and how it makes you feel.

My score for my goal is:

_____

My thoughts on that score:

_____

_____

_____

5. WHAT WERE THE GAPS TO ACHIEVING YOUR GOAL?

Overall, if you didn't achieve as much as you wanted to, was there anything that stopped it from happening? Could you have allocated more time to coaching over the three months? Did something unexpected happen as you were going through the process? Were you under-resourced? Like Mike, could you have spent less time at the start of the coaching clouded by a negative attitude towards others?

My gaps between me and the goal were:

_____

_____

_____

_____

6. WHAT DID YOU LEARN ABOUT YOURSELF?

The way you go for your goals is often a reflection of the way you approach anything that is important to you in your life. This is highlighted in the coaching process because you are looking to achieve new things in three months. Now that you have been through this experience what have you noticed about yourself? Do you thrive on stress? Are you not so good at time management? Do you need to ask for help more? Are you an inspiration to others? Have you moved ahead faster than you ever thought possible? Do you have more skills or resources than you would have credited? Write down at least five things that you now know about yourself.

1. _____

   _____

2. _____

   _____

3. _____

   _____

4. _____

   _____

5. _____

   _____

Congratulations – you have completed the entire process. That brings us to the end of the coaching. Hopefully after spending time on the above actions you now feel a sense of completion about the work you have done over the last 12 weeks of your life. Wherever you are right now is absolutely the right place for you to be in.

What's Next?

Now that you've completed the 12 steps of the course, what's next? Through going for your goal, it's likely you have developed some great new habits. Now is the time to create a way to ensure your new habits stay with you. Keep on applying what you have learned. For example, if your goal was around building your business, through the coaching you may have created smarter systems for making profit or running the business more efficiently. Document these new systems, take the time to teach them to current and new employees, find ways to set new minimum targets so that the new profit level is maintained. Keep your vision alive by putting your employees through a coaching program. Imagine having one person at all times in coaching – what a difference that could make to a small business.

If you find yourself getting stuck back in the same rut as before you went through this process, take the time to look back over the great work you did in the past 90 days. Perhaps looking over your vision ('Bring Your Goal To Life') will provide you with inspiration. Or maybe you're not giving yourself adequate support to get what you want ('Plan For Success'). One of the best ways you can continue to achieve what you want is to set time aside each week to relive what you achieved in the goal area last time, to have an ongoing one hour per week to keep your goals alive.

Another choice may be to set yourself a new goal and start back at the beginning of the book. That is the real beauty of this system – it really can be applied to anything. If you are finding that you have more time to allocate towards getting what you want, try using the system outlined to work on two or three goals at the same time. Be aware that this will take a much higher degree of discipline and more time.

If you decide to work with a real coach, you'll be tackling three big goals at once, not just one. So if you really want to ramp up your success, it might be time to call upon a coach for yourself.

GETTING YOUR OWN PROFESSIONAL LIFE COACH

Following the exercises in this book is obviously not exactly the same as having a life coach. However, from this book you may have had a glimpse of what having a coach could do for you. Perhaps you want to explore this a little further now. If so, there is an easy way to do that. There are hundreds of Results coaches in Australia, New Zealand, the US and the UK, and many more sprouting up in other regions of the world all the time. The best way to find the one closest to you is to just go to the Results website. There you can see all the Accredited Life Coaches worldwide in one place. The address is: www.ResultsCoaches.com

All Results Life Coaches are available via email to answer a question, give you feedback or have a quick chat to help you with an issue.

On the website you'll see a photo and a summary of what each coach has to offer. There is a great range of ages, backgrounds and personalities to choose from. It is important to remember that it is not essential for a life coach to have experience in the areas that you set your goals. As you have seen from this book, the Results coaching system is flexible enough to adapt to any goal and all of the coaches have been trained to support clients in all of the goal areas.

So, what do you need to ask yourself when choosing a life coach? You will be paying this person to help you reach your goals so you have a right to be discerning. Do you know that you respond better to direction from a man or a woman? Do you relate better to someone closer to your own age? Are you looking for a perspective that will only be given to you by your complete opposite? Keep these kinds of questions in mind when you look through the website to see if any of the coaches appeal. Alternatively you can phone your nearest Results office and describe the qualities you want in a life coach and they will do their best to find that person for you. Another option is to email several coaches and conduct a mini interview to help you make your choice.

The best way to know whether coaching will work for you is to do what we call a 'trial session' with a coach. For this first session you are under no obligation to take on that specific coach or a coaching series at the end of the 75 minutes.

During the trial session you will have a conversation with the coach regarding what life coaching is about, how the series will run and, most importantly, you will set three really inspiring goals for yourself. Results coaches are very well trained in setting 'goals worth going for', and you will walk out of the session clearer on where you want to go, with three fantastic goals to give you some direction for the next three months, whether or not you decide to take on the coach.

Books And Other Resources For All Types Of Goals

These books are the ones that Results coaches use and recommend when working with clients. They can often be a valuable addition to your coaching journey. Most of the books are readily available so just go to your local book store, or you can order these from our website, www.ResultsCoaches.com. The site also has some interesting Internet resources for many of the goal areas.

FINANCIAL GOALS

Napoleon Hill & Melvin Powers, *Think and Grow Rich*, Wilshire, USA, 1999

Robert Kiyosaki, *Cashflow Quadrant*, Warner Books, USA, 2000

Robert Kiyosaki, *Rich Dad, Poor Dad*, Warner Books, USA, 2000

Suze Orman, *The 9 Steps to Financial Freedom*, Three Rivers Press, USA, 2000

BUSINESS GOALS

Kenneth Blanchard & Spencer Johnson, *The One Minute Manager*, Berkeley Publishing Group, USA, 1993

James C. Collins & Jerry I. Porras, *Built To Last*, Harper Business, USA, 1997

Michael E. Gerber, *The E-Myth Revisited*, HarperCollins, USA, 1995

Al Ries & Jack Trout, *The 22 Immutable Laws of Marketing*, Harper Business, USA, 1994

RELATIONSHIP GOALS

John Gray, *Men are From Mars, Women Are From Venus*, HarperCollins, USA, 1992

Phil McGraw, *Relationship Rescue: A Seven-Step Strategy for Reconnecting with Your Partner*, Hyperion, USA, 2000

HEALTH GOALS

Dr Sandra Cabot, *The Liver-Cleansing Diet*, Ten Speed Press, USA, 1998

Daniel P. Reid, *The Tao of Health, Sex and Longevity*, Fireside, USA, 1989

Andrew Weil, *Natural Health, Natural Medicine*, Houghton Mifflin Co., USA, 1998

PERSONAL GOALS

Dr Wayne Dyer, *You'll See it When You Believe It*, Avon, USA, 1990

Daniel Goleman, *Emotional Intelligence*, Bloomsbury Paperbacks, USA, 1998

David Niven PhD, *The 100 Simple Secrets of Happy People*, HarperCollins, USA, 2000

M. Scott Peck, *The Road Less Travelled*, Simon & Schuster, USA, 1997

Cheryl Richardson, *Life Makeovers*, Broadway Books, USA, 2000

Sark, *Succulent Wild Woman: Dancing with your Wonder Full Self*, Fireside, USA, 1997

CAREER

Laurence G. Boldt, *Zen and the Art of Making a Living*, Penguin, USA, 1999

Richard Nelson Bolles & Dick Bolles, *What Colour Is Your Parachute?*, Ten Speed Press, USA, 2001

Stephen Covey, *The 7 Habits of Highly Effective People*, Simon & Schuster, USA, 1998

Laura Berman Fortgang, *Take Yourself to the Top*, Warner Books, USA, 1998

Barbara Sher, *Wishcraft*, Ballantine Books, USA 1986

CREATIVE GOALS

Julia Cameron, *The Artist's Way*, Macmillan Publishers, UK, 1992

Roland Fishman, *The Book of Creative Wisdom*, Random House, Australia, 2000

BECOME A COACH OR FIND A COACH
www.ResultsCoaches.com

BRINGING COACHING INTO YOUR ORGANISATION
www.resultslifecoaching.com.au/corporate/corporateindex.html

PROFESSIONAL COACHING ASSOCIATIONS
International Coaching Federation – www.coachfederation.org

Personal Lifestyle Checklist

This is a checklist all Results life coaches do with clients at the start of a coaching journey, and then at the start of each month after that. It's a great way of seeing where you are stronger and weaker in your life, and looking for ways to get more of a solid foundation to live from. Simply tick a box for each point, either true of false. The idea is to have as many in the 'true' column as possible.

T F

WORK
☐ ☐ My work stimulates me
☐ ☐ I am proud of what I do for a job
☐ ☐ I feel appreciated at work
☐ ☐ I respect my co-workers
☐ ☐ I know where my career is heading
☐ ☐ My boss is aware of where I want my career to go and supports that
☐ ☐ I complete my work within reasonable hours
☐ ☐ I respond to phone calls and emails within 48 hours and don't let paperwork pile up too long
☐ ☐ I manage my time well
☐ ☐ I delegate without guilt

FINANCES
☐ ☐ I am satisfied with my income
☐ ☐ I have a budget that I use
☐ ☐ I pay my bills on time
☐ ☐ I know how much I owe and when it will be paid off
☐ ☐ I have an active long-term financial plan
☐ ☐ I am able to reward myself without feeling guilty
☐ ☐ I use my credit card wisely
☐ ☐ I have a will

T F

- ☐ ☐ My wallet is uncluttered
- ☐ ☐ My tax affairs are up to date

HOME ENVIRONMENT

- ☐ ☐ I am happy with my home
- ☐ ☐ My home is generally clean and tidy
- ☐ ☐ I surround myself with things that I love
- ☐ ☐ I don't acquire clutter
- ☐ ☐ I recycle at home
- ☐ ☐ My personal files are in order
- ☐ ☐ My bed supports me having a good sleep
- ☐ ☐ My bed is always properly made
- ☐ ☐ I have photos of loved ones on display
- ☐ ☐ I am happy with my mode of transport

HEALTH AND BODY

- ☐ ☐ I am happy with my current weight
- ☐ ☐ I do some form of exercise at least three times a week
- ☐ ☐ I have a balanced diet including lots of fresh food
- ☐ ☐ I don't smoke or drink alcohol excessively
- ☐ ☐ I drink at least 2 litres of water every day
- ☐ ☐ I am up to date with all necessary medical and dental check-ups
- ☐ ☐ I am happy with the sleep I get
- ☐ ☐ I have appropriate clothes for my work and personal interests
- ☐ ☐ I am not concerned about my stress levels
- ☐ ☐ I feel generally well

RELATIONSHIPS

- ☐ ☐ I am happy with the level of intimacy in my life
- ☐ ☐ My partner and I respect each other and are equals
- ☐ ☐ I get along well with my work colleagues
- ☐ ☐ I make amends easily with people I have had conflicts with
- ☐ ☐ I trust the significant people in my life
- ☐ ☐ I am on good speaking terms with my neighbours
- ☐ ☐ I consider myself to be a good friend

T F

❑ ❑ I see people who are important to me regularly

❑ ❑ My friends and family know how much I care about them

❑ ❑ I am satisfied with my social life

PERSONAL

❑ ❑ I like myself

❑ ❑ I have had a birthday party in the last two years

❑ ❑ I have a life outside of my work

❑ ❑ I have enough confidence to do what I want in life

❑ ❑ I have adequate holidays each year

❑ ❑ I don't lie or exaggerate

❑ ❑ I am comfortable saying 'no' when I need to

❑ ❑ People know they can count on me to do what I say
I will do

❑ ❑ I can easily recall the last time I really laughed

❑ ❑ I have a form of creative expression

Becoming A Life Coach

I am sure many people reading this book will come to the end and realise coaching is just what they want to do for a profession. If this is you, I have captured a little bit of information on the subject here as an introduction. However, the best way to get more information is to go to the Results website and get details about free information evenings close to you.

Firstly, here are the main benefits of becoming a coach.

FULFILLMENT
Most people have probably had some sort of experience of coaching other people. It's those times when you say something to someone, and you just know their whole life will be altered somehow. Don't these moments feel amazing? Well, imagine being paid to do this every day. Many coaches say this is the most rewarding work they have ever done. It's hard to beat helping people realise their potential as a fulfilling career.

PERSONAL DEVELOPMENT
There is no need to go to weekend courses or volunteer your time when your career is linked to personal development. Part of the requirement in being a coach is being a powerful and inspiring human being, someone that other people want to be around. This is supported by every Results life coach having at least one coaching series per year, where they get to focus on enhancing their lives and achieving their own goals. Being a professional coach is a great structure for having your life become inspiring and to be constantly challenged to learn and grow.

FLEXIBILITY
Coaching is one of the most flexible careers there is. You can do it from anywhere, at times to suit you. Many coaches choose to work from a home office and it can easily be balanced with another career. You can take advantage of scheduling clients at times that

you know you work at your peak. You can build your business up to a level you want as you want to. You can also schedule time off for yourself, take extended leave or work in other countries without affecting the success of your coaching career.

INCOME

Your income as a coach depends on the type of clients you have and the fees that you negotiate with each client individually. There are three different levels of clients as determined by the goals they set: personal, small business and executive goals, from $60 up to $250 per hour. Additionally there are also all the tax benefits that anyone is entitled to when running a business from home. It can be a lucrative option as a part-time job or a full-time career.

HOW YOU BECOME A COACH

First of all, you need to be a client before you start. At Results, we require that people have their own coach for at least one month prior to starting a training course.

Secondly you need to fill out an application form. You can download one off the Web at www.ResultsCoaches.com. There is a peer review as well as some personal questions. Not all applicants are accepted into a training program. Results requires evidence of strong existing interpersonal skills and a high level of personal awareness and responsibility.

The training course is roughly 12 months long in total and is delivered both face to face in several locations as well as by remote teleconference training, for people everywhere. Results offers face-to-face training in most states in Australia at least once a year, and now in the US in New Jersey, with other regions in the US opening shortly.

The Future Of Coaching

Coaching is fast becoming a stand-alone profession worldwide. Its roots lie in fields such as training, mentoring, management, personal development and counselling, but its future lies as an independent and clearly defined profession.

Ten years ago there were only a handful of coaches in the US; now there are around 15,000 coaches there. The *Sydney Morning Herald* in February 1999 said that personal coaching was the second-fastest growth industry in the US after information technology.

At the beginning of 1996 there were less than half a dozen coaches in Australia. At December 2000 there are over 400. My personal belief is there will be around 3000–4000 coaches in Australia by 2005, about as many as there are pharmacies, or a handful in every suburb. I think it will be the same for most modern Western countries. Results Life Coaching intends to be a major part of this future, opening training and support centres in each capital city in Australia in the next five years, and then establishing franchises around the world.

Coaching is now being picked up by corporations worldwide as a performance tool for high-potential individuals and as a resource for helping senior staff maintain a more healthy work–life balance. There are now hundreds of major firms in the US hiring coaches for their CEOs, senior executives and middle management. Australia is following close behind this pattern.

There is already a strong global professional resource for coaching, the International Coaching Federation, which is now in Australia as well. The ICF provides a forum for building professionalism in the industry, including maintaining professional standards and ethics, a credentialling program and a rich set of competencies for coaching. It also has a conference every year in the US, attended now by thousands of coaches each year. For more information go to www.coachfederation.org.